DAVE FLYNN

Complete Works for Solo Guitar

I0808826

Visit us at www.melbay.com — E-mail us at email@melbay.com

Contents

FOREWORD by Charles Postlewate

It is an honor, a privilege and my sincere pleasure to offer a prelude to this publication of Irish composer Dave Flynn's complete collection, to date, of his works for solo guitar. The music of Dave Flynn reflects the compositonal style of a well trained and experienced composer who has assimilated the language and style of the many fine classical composers he has studied, from the contrapuntal music of the Baroque period to the minimalist, contemporary composers who have influenced, but not stifled, his style. Dave's music is tonal with elements of extended harmonies from the world of jazz, and contains rhythms and melodies that would be expected from a musician who has matured, developed, and prospered under the canopy of Irish folk music. With influences also from around the modern world's wide variety of popular and ethnic music, Dave Flynn's music is many things, but never mundane, and deserves to be known and recognized by a large audience in the guitar world.

I first became acquainted with Dave's music while compiling for Mel Bay Publications my *Contemporary Anthology of Solo Guitar Music for Five Fingers of the Right Hand* (MB21290), published in 2009. I found the writings of Dave Flynn to be a refreshing combination of contemporary musical language with the beautiful melodies and vibrant rhythms of his native Ireland. And, most important to me, his music used a contemporary technique that makes full use of the capabilities of all five fingers of the right hand. Similar to the music of Heitor Villa-Lobos (1887-1959), whose music was also conceived for five fingers of the right hand, Dave's compositions can be played without the use of the right-hand little finger, but it sure makes life easier for the guitarist who decides to use that *extra* finger. Or, in the immortal words of Villa-Lobos in 1924: "You don't use your little finger? Then cut it off! Cut it off!"

I sincerely hope that this publication will expand the growing recognition that Dave Flynn truly merits. And here's hoping that you, the performer, enjoy the music of this fine musician as much as I have savored it over the past ten years. While this is a complete collection to *date*, I anticipate that Dave Flynn's collection will continue to grow with more of his opuses to enrich our contemporary guitar literature.

Charles Postlewate
Granbury, Texas, USA
December 23, 2018

*Author's note - Charles Postlewate kindly wrote this foreword for my book just a few months before he passed away. News of his passing came as a great shock to me as I had been in email contact with him shortly beforehand and he was in good spirits. Charles was a kind, generous man and a ground-breaking contributor to the classical guitar world.

I dedicate this book to his memory.

INTRODUCTION by Dave Flynn

Thank you so much for your interest in my guitar works. It is always a leap into the unknown to play new music, so I am delighted you are taking that leap with my music. The compositions presented here include all of the solo guitar pieces I had written as of 2018. They range from the first classical piece I wrote at age 16, "Elegy for Joan", to "The Mahatma of the Glen" from my 2009 album *Contemporary Traditional Irish Guitar*. I have created more solo guitar works since, such as "An Irish Raga" and my 2014 album *Winter Variations;* however, these are not included here as they are improvisations rather than notated compositions.

My style developed significantly in the 16 years between "Elegy for Joan" and "The Mahatma of the Glen". Early pieces are strongly influenced by certain composers, hence the "Homage Sonatina" name-checks Heitor Villa-Lobos, Leo Brouwer and Andy Summers. "The Three Gymn O'Paddies" are obviously influenced by Erik Satie, yet my 'Irishness' began to show here as they are the first pieces in which I brought in subtle elements from Irish folk music.

When I entered music college in 1999 I became exposed to contemporary American minimalist composers Steve Reich, John Adams and Philip Glass. None of them had composed solo works for guitar, so I was inspired by their example to create some minimalist guitar pieces, "5 to 9" being perhaps the best example in this collection. I entered Neo-Baroque territory with "Passacaglia" (2000), the most technically difficult piece in the collection. I particularly enjoy "Passacaglia" and "5 to 9".

An unusual aspect of both those pieces is that I use the little finger of my plucking hand a few times to create a sharp upward arpeggio. I find the little finger gives a special kind of snap that other fingers cannot duplicate. A few years later I read an article about the American guitarist Charles Postlewate who developed a complete five-finger plucking-hand technique and wrote a tutorial about it. Fascinated, I contacted him and this led to him asking me to compose some music for an anthology of new works he was preparing. The "Etudes for Five Fingers" are the result of this. The first four were originally published by Mel Bay Publications in Charles' *Contemporary Anthology of Solo Guitar Music for Five Fingers of the Right-Hand* (MB21290).

Stylistically these etudes merge ideas from minimalism, Irish folk and jazz. They hint at my future direction as a composer of cross-genre orchestral music. A few years later I rediscovered sketches of two other etudes* I had been working on in 2000 and completed them. They transfer some of Philip Glass' early minimalist techniques to the guitar but with some jazz harmony.

*No. 5 "The Glass Harp" and No. 6 "The Glass Abacus"

Six Etudes for Five Fingers

I composed the first four of these etudes for Charles Postlewate to aid his pioneering work utilizing the five-finger plucking-hand technique. Each is designed to aid the development of separate techniques using the little finger of the plucking hand. I am very sympathetic to Charles' ideas because I have used the little finger in my playing and in some of my other compositions. These pieces were previously published by Mel Bay Publications in the *Contemporary Anthology of Solo Guitar Music for Five Fingers of the Right Hand* (MBP21290). There are some small changes to the etudes in this new publication. I have also added two more etudes which I rediscovered in my sketches. The sketches date from 2000 and I completed them in 2011. These etudes are influenced by Philip Glass' minimalist techniques.

Etude No. 1: "Gimme Five" is mainly concerned with the development of arpeggios utilizing the little finger, notated here as *'c'* [for *cuarto* (fourth) in Spanish]. The 5/8 time signature is used because it naturally fits the five fingers in a way that will make an unusual rhythm for guitar students seem quite natural. Early exposure to irregular time signatures will aid the student's development and they will come as naturally to the advanced student as the five-finger technique. I have encountered many technically-advanced players who find irregular time signatures difficult due to the lack of exposure in early training. The piece should be very atmospheric with particular attention paid to the fermatas. They should be held long enough to allow the harmonics of each chord to be clearly audible.

Etude No. 2: "Homage to Bucko" is concerned with one of the main advantages of the five-finger technique – unbroken five-note chords. The piece should be accessible to most players, although some players may wish to end the piece at bar 20 until they have developed the left hand enough to tackle some of the chords in the rest of the piece. The piece should build to a majestic climax. The last chord is sounded by a sharp up-stroke with the *c* finger, beginning on the first string. When the *c* finger reaches the fourth string the thumb sounds the bass-note A. This technique can also be found in my pieces "5 to 9" and "Passacaglia". Jazz harmonies influence this piece. I wrote it in homage to the renowned jazz guitarist Hugh Buckley, who helped develop my interest in jazz.

Etude No. 3: "The Odd Reel" is a steppingstone to a fluid tremolo utilizing the little finger. This is not a continuous tremolo in the manner of Tárrega and Barrios; rather, there is more of a relation to the *treble* ornament found in Irish folk music. A treble usually consists of three notes of the same pitch played rapidly. The first two notes of a treble sometimes have a percussive, muted sound. This percussive treble was a particular trait of the fiddle player and composer Tommy Peoples. If played at a moderate pace the piece is accessible to most players, while more advanced players are encouraged to play the piece faster to develop the technique. In performance, I prefer the piece to be played at a moderate tempo. Irish jigs and reels can be played at vastly differing tempi, depending on the players and the regional style, so the tempo really is up to the individual. Ornaments should be played in a manner similar to Irish traditional music ornaments. I recommend listening to fiddle players like Martin Hayes and Paddy Glackin to get the general spirit of the piece and a better understanding of how to play these ornaments. Please also refer to the ornamentation guide provided on page 16.

Etude No. 4: "Static Slip Jig" is based upon the traditional Irish slip jig rhythm in 9/8 time (3+3+3) and, because the 9/8 feel of a slip jig is quite different than that of a Baroque gigue, I recommend listening to recordings of slip jigs to get the right feel for this piece. Good examples include Kevin Burke and Míchéal Ó Domhnaill performing the title track of their album *Promenade* and The Bothy Band playing "The Butterfly" on their album *1975*. This etude will help develop the dexterity of the right hand. The relationship between the thumb and all four fingers will be developed, as will the relationship of *c* to *a*, *a* to *m,* and *m* to *i*.

Etude No. 5: "The Glass Harp" is a combination of harp-like *campanellas* and minimalist techniques pioneered by Philip Glass in the late 1960s and early 1970s. The harmonic material deviates from his style though as it is quite jazz-influenced. I have not added any fingerings, dynamics, or timbre directions as I like this piece to be completely open to interpretation. This spare approach to notation is quite idiomatic of early Philip Glass works. It is nevertheless possible to make this a very effective study piece for five-finger technique if the *c* finger is used.

Etude No. 6: "The Glass Abacus" has a similarly free approach to fingering, dynamics, and timbre. It also has jazz-influenced harmonies. The difference with the previous etude is in the rhythms. Here I use Philip Glass' technique of additive and subtractive time signatures, whereby a pattern is repeated and notes get added or taken away to create gradually changing time signatures. This makes it an excellent study piece, especially if the *c* finger is used.

Three Gymn O'Paddies

These pieces have roughly the same form as Erik Satie's "Three Gymnopedies" (1888). The punning title of my pieces betrays the Irish character found in the melodies. This is particularly evident in the ornamentation, which should be played as described in the ornamentation guide. In concert, the pieces can be spread apart between other works for variety as they all have the same general style. The guitarist Philip Lawson was the first to intersperse these pieces with others in performance, and I thought it worked nicely.

Homage Sonatina

The movements of the "Homage Sonatina" were originally written as separate pieces. I decided to combine them in sonatina form when I realized they were all written in homage to composer/guitarists, namely Heitor Villa-Lobos, Andy Summers and Leo Brouwer.

I - "Homage to Heitor Villa-Lobos" – Villa-Lobos, one of the great composers for the guitar, was the first major 20th Century composer I seriously studied. I wrote this piece through improvisation. On completion I realized it owed a debt to Villa-Lobos, so I acknowledged this by naming the piece after him. Aside from this influence, there are some jazz elements.

II - "Elegy for Joan (Homage to Andy Summers)" – This is the first piece I wrote in a contemporary classical style; it is also the first piece I wrote in standard notation. The original title of the piece was "Homage to Andy Summers". Andy Summers is best known as the guitarist in the rock group *The Police.* His playing had an enormous influence on me in my teenage years. He incorporated many different genres in his playing to create a truly innovative style. Some of the chords he commonly used with *The Police* are found in the piece, such as the first Aadd9 chord. In 2001 my mother Joan Jennings died, so I decided to rename the piece in her honor, as, among my compositions, it was one of her favorite works.

III - "Irish Seascapes with Waves (Homage to Leo Brouwer)" – This piece is a play on Leo Brouwer's "Cuban Landscape" series. It is my tribute to Mr. Brouwer, one of the great guitarist/ composers. The ending has some unusual percussive effects, which are explained in the notation guide at the start of the piece.

Passacaglia

This piece is faithful to the Baroque passacaglia form where there is a constant ostinato, mostly in the bass, but occasionally in higher registers. This is probably the darkest piece in the collection; it should be performed with a sense of evil or darkness, with great emphasis on dissonances and the special effects. I wrote this as a composition student at the Dublin Conservatory of Music and Drama. We were assigned a task to create a piece based on a musical alphabet. I devised an alphabet and, in the spirit of J. S. Bach and Shostakovich, some melodies in the piece are derived from versions of my name as found in my alphabet. The theme that opens the piece is one such 'name melody'. The notes D, F, G♯, A, B, B spell out D FLYNN in my alphabet. Another name melody appears in bar 43 with the notes D, A, D♯, C, D spelling out DAVID. The structure of the alphabet is something I prefer to keep mysterious. A good mathematician should be able to work it out from those name-melody clues!

Below are explanations of some numbered passages;

1. In bar 31 the notes should be allowed to ring like bells (*a la campanas).*
2. The chords in bars 37-39 should all be plucked, i.e., played portamento not glissando.
3. Bars 55-56 have glissandi which are meant to be sardonic and clownish. The glissandi in bar 56 are in imitation of a wolf whistle. A wolf whistle is attributed particularly to male construction workers from the 1970s and 1980s who used to commonly whistle at attractive women passing by.
4. In bars 61-62 the notes should be slurred as smoothly and evenly as possible, with only the first note of each tuplet plucked.
5. Bars 64-66 require a special technique whereby the performer rapidly arpeggiates all notes with the finger indicated, i.e., *c* or *i,* except the accented bass notes, which should be firmly played by the thumb. When executed properly, the *c* or *i* finger should reach the last note of its arpeggio at the same time as the thumb plucks the bass note. If the performer has an inadequate *c* finger (i.e., if it is too short or has no nail) then it is permissible to use *a.* It is vital to the unique sound of this section to follow the tonal qualities exactly, i.e., go gradually from *ponticello* to *tasto* and back.

The Mahatma of the Glen

Again dedicated to my mother's memory, this piece has its origins in a 2006 suite, for Irish fiddle, classical violin and guitar, called *Music for the Departed,* a musical portrait of the seven stages of the grieving process. In 2009 I arranged three sections from *Music for the Departed* for solo guitar in honor of the great Irish fiddle player James Byrne, after he passed away suddenly. I had gotten to know James from visits to his home area of Glencolmkille in Donegal. I had the privilege of learning from him and playing with him. His death affected a lot of people deeply, including myself, as he was a wonderful man, musician and teacher who had memorized a huge store of folk music. When he died, some of that music left with him. Luckily he taught a lot of music to younger generations, thus saving a tradition. At his funeral the priest called him "The Mahatma of the Glen", so I used that beautifully apt title for this piece.

"The Mahatma of the Glen" begins with "Grief", a slow air that can be played very freely and mournfully. It is not important to adhere to bar lengths and time signatures.

"Tears" is in the 12/8 rhythm of a type of Irish jig called a *slide*. Slides are usually played very quickly, however this slide should be played quite slowly. There should not be any rubato; it needs a steady pulse, as is common for all dance-based Irish folk music.

"Nostalgia" is a livelier and unusual kind of jig that I've christened a 'slip-slide', as it mixes the 9/8 of a slip jig with the 12/8 of a slide. Again, there should be no rubato, except for the ritardando.

I recorded "The Mahatma of the Glen" on my 2009 album *Contemporary Traditional Irish Guitar*. If you listen to that recording you will notice there are quite a few melodic and rhythmic differences in the music I have notated here. The reason for this is that Irish folk music is somewhat improvisational and this piece is a modern take on Irish folk music. Melodic and rhythmic variations are an important part of the Irish folk tradition, so I never play this piece the same way twice. The version printed here is just one possible way to play it. I encourage performers to learn about the principles of variation and ornamentation in Irish folk music. Once a good understanding of these is attained, it is possible to tastefully vary this piece from the written notation.

If you wish to play this piece, even exactly as notated, please pay particular attention to the ornamentation guide because the ornaments in this piece are quite different from classical ornaments. They are also a good deal harder to articulate than the notation suggests!

When I play this piece I use an alternative tuning - DADGAE. By dropping the B string to A, I can emulate some open-string ornaments that Irish fiddle players use. The piece can be played with normal tuning and is easier to play that way, but I do not think it is as effective. It's up to you to choose which tuning you want to use.

Irish Folk Ornamentation Guide

There are Irish folk ornaments in the 'Three Gymn O'Paddies', 'Etudes 3 & 4' and 'The Mahatma of the Glen'. Do not mistake them for classical grace notes. The pitch of the ornaments should not be audible.
All such ornaments are thirty-second notes with crossed note-heads.
I have notated two kinds of Irish ornaments in the pieces; Cuts and Rolls.

1. Cuts

Cuts are rapid articulations of the main notes which come almost on the beat of the main note. They are sounded with a quick flick of the fretting finger.

a.) b.) c.) d.)

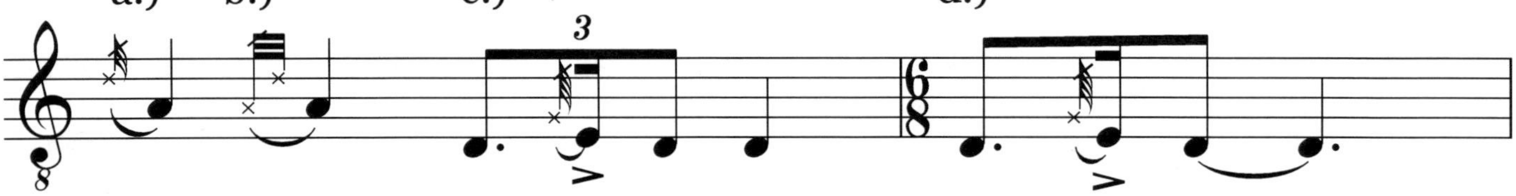

2. Rolls

Rolls are commonly used in the space of a triplet or three eighth notes.
There are many variations on the roll. The key to getting a roll correct is to very rapidly articulate the main notes with the left hand fingers.
Always ensure the principal note is the only one clearly heard.
Various rolls are notated in 'The Mahatma of the Glen'. You can vary which rolls you use throughout the piece, below are some to choose from.
Rolls are not idiomatic to the guitar, they take LOTS of practice to get right!
Listen to how I do them on my album 'Contemporary Traditional Irish Guitar'.

a.) Standard Roll b.) Sliding Roll c.) Rapid Roll d.) Treble Roll

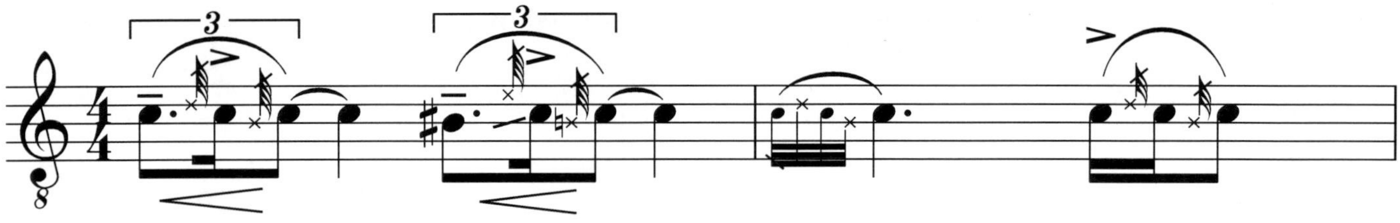

e.) Standard Roll variations f.) 6/8 version g.) 6/8 version

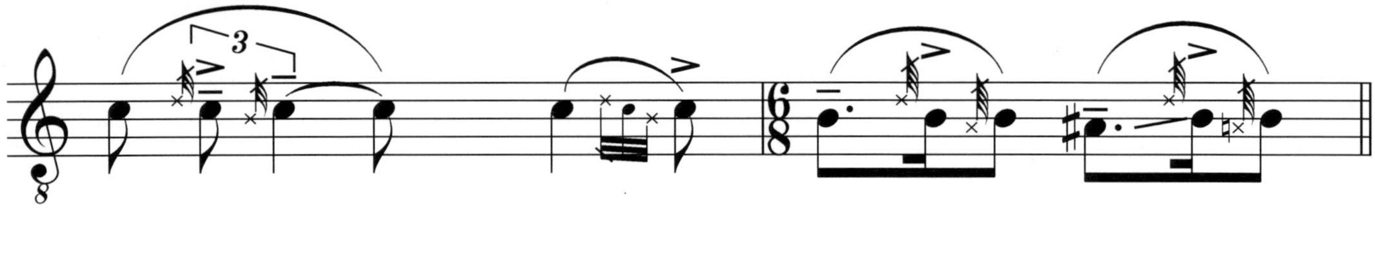

Three Minimalist Pieces (1998-2000)

I 5 to 9

II Rainstorm

III Rollercoaster

THREE MINIMALIST PIECES

I

Allegro

5 to 9

Dave Flynn
Dublin, April 2000

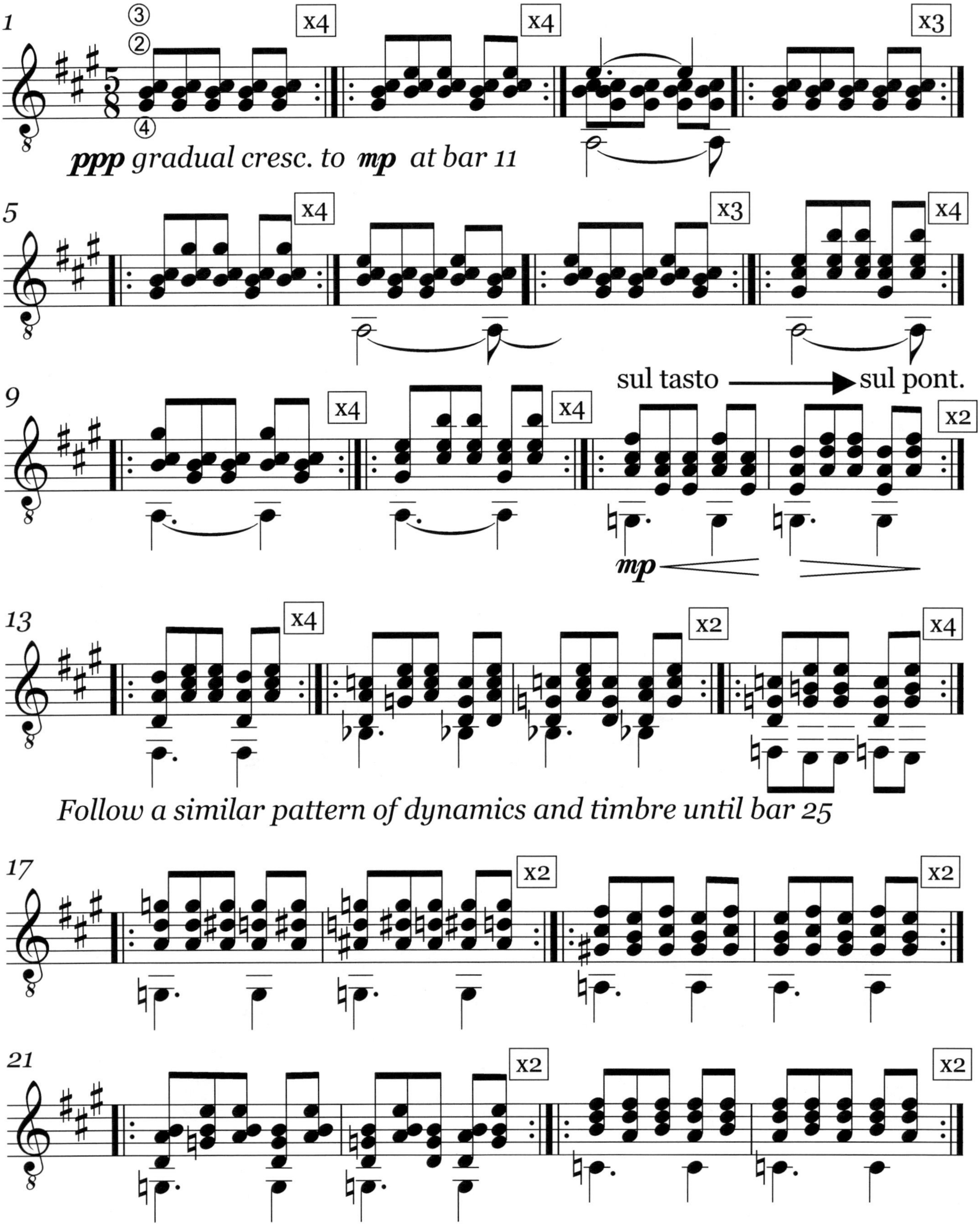

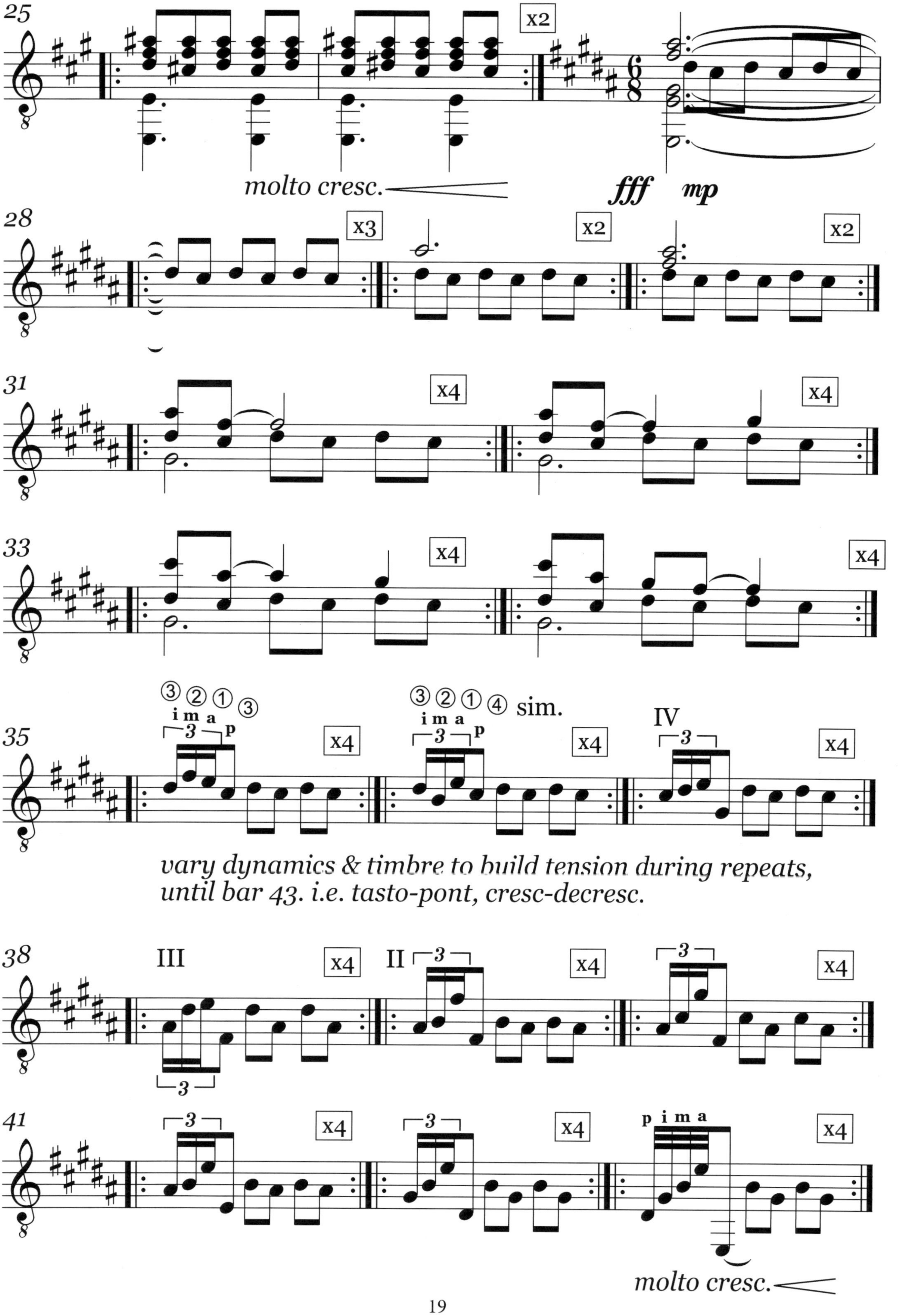
25
x2
molto cresc.
fff
mp
28
x3
x2
x2
31
x4
x4
33
x4
x4
35
i m a
p
x4
sim.
x4
IV
x4
vary dynamics & timbre to build tension during repeats,
until bar 43. i.e. tasto-pont, cresc-decresc.
38
III
x4
II
x4
x4
41
x4
x4
p i m a
x4
molto cresc.

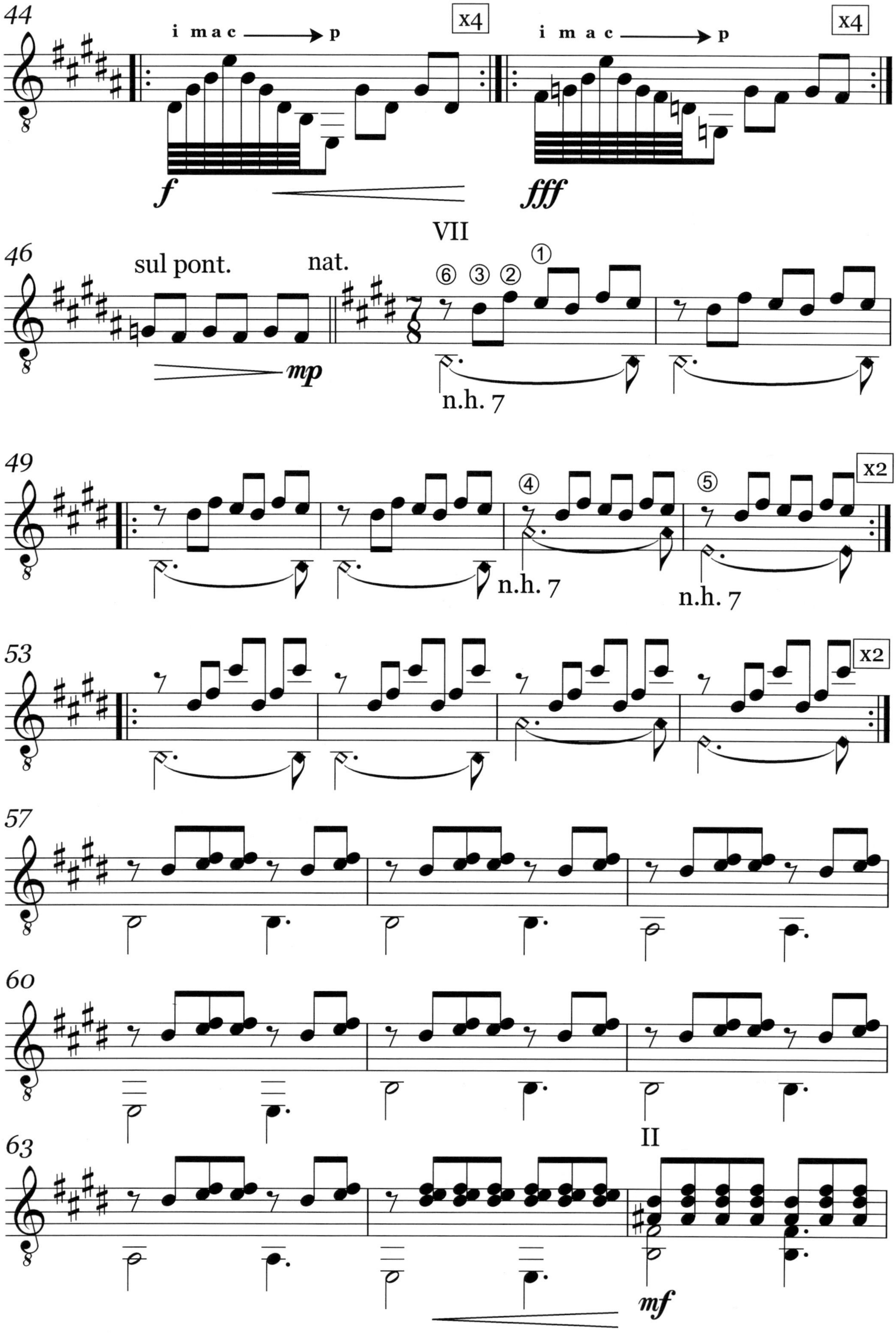
44
i m a c p
x4
f
fff
46
sul pont.
nat.
mp
VII
n.h. 7
49
x2
53
57
60
63
II
mf

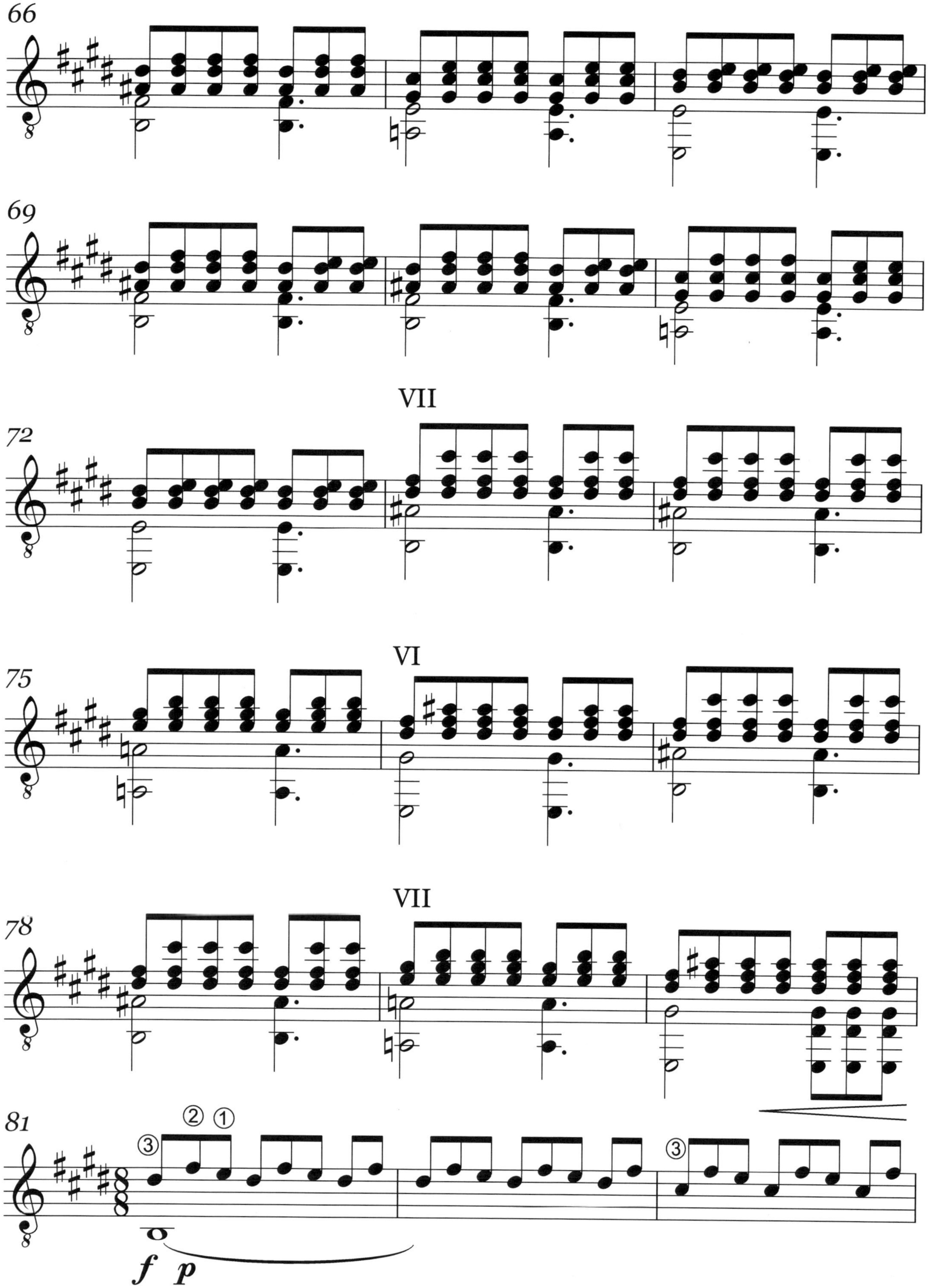
66
69
VII
72
VI
75
VII
78
81
③ ② ①
③
f p

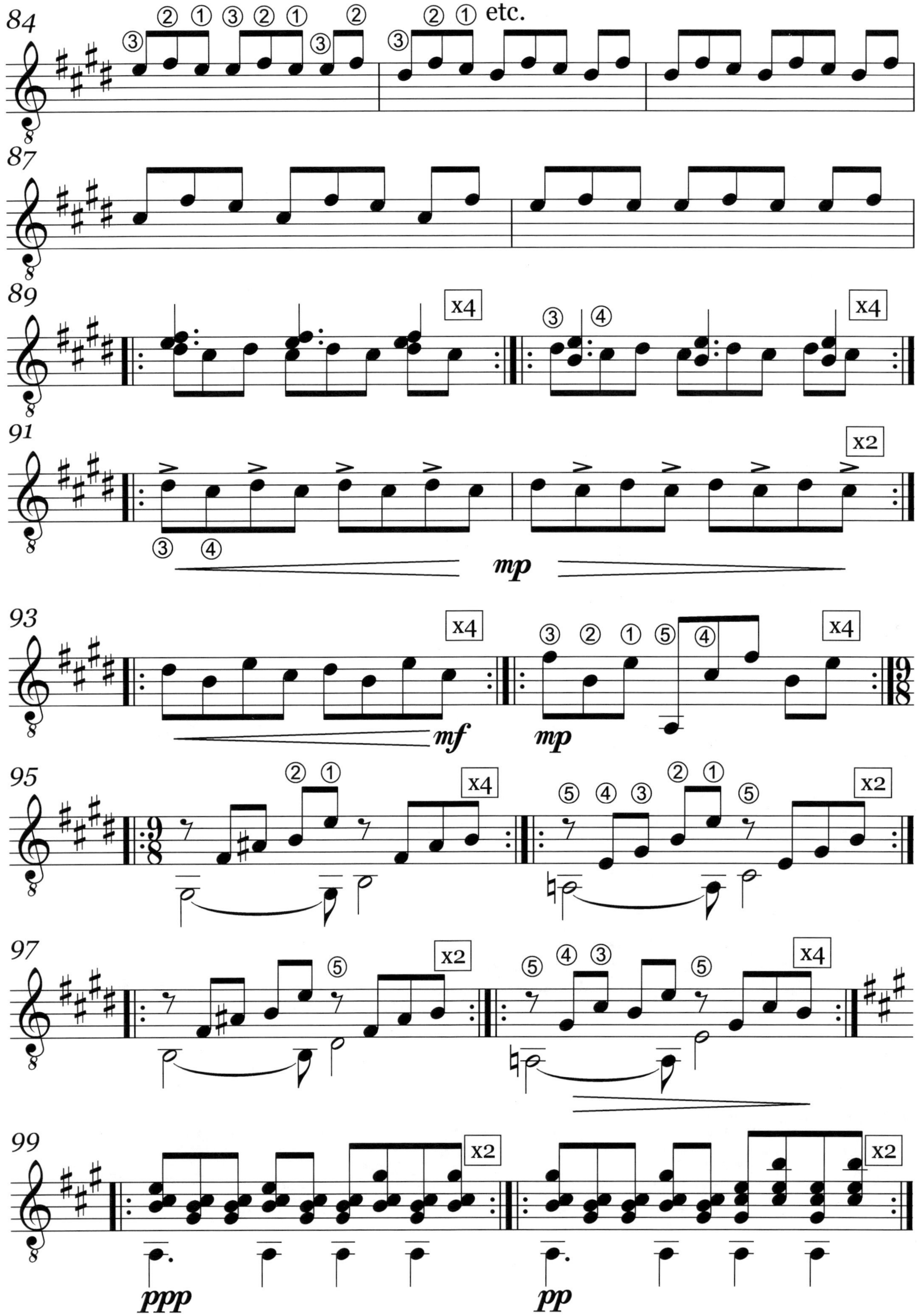
84
etc.
87
89
x4
x4
91
x2
mp
93
x4
x4
mf
mp
95
x4
x2
97
x2
x4
99
x2
x2
ppp
pp

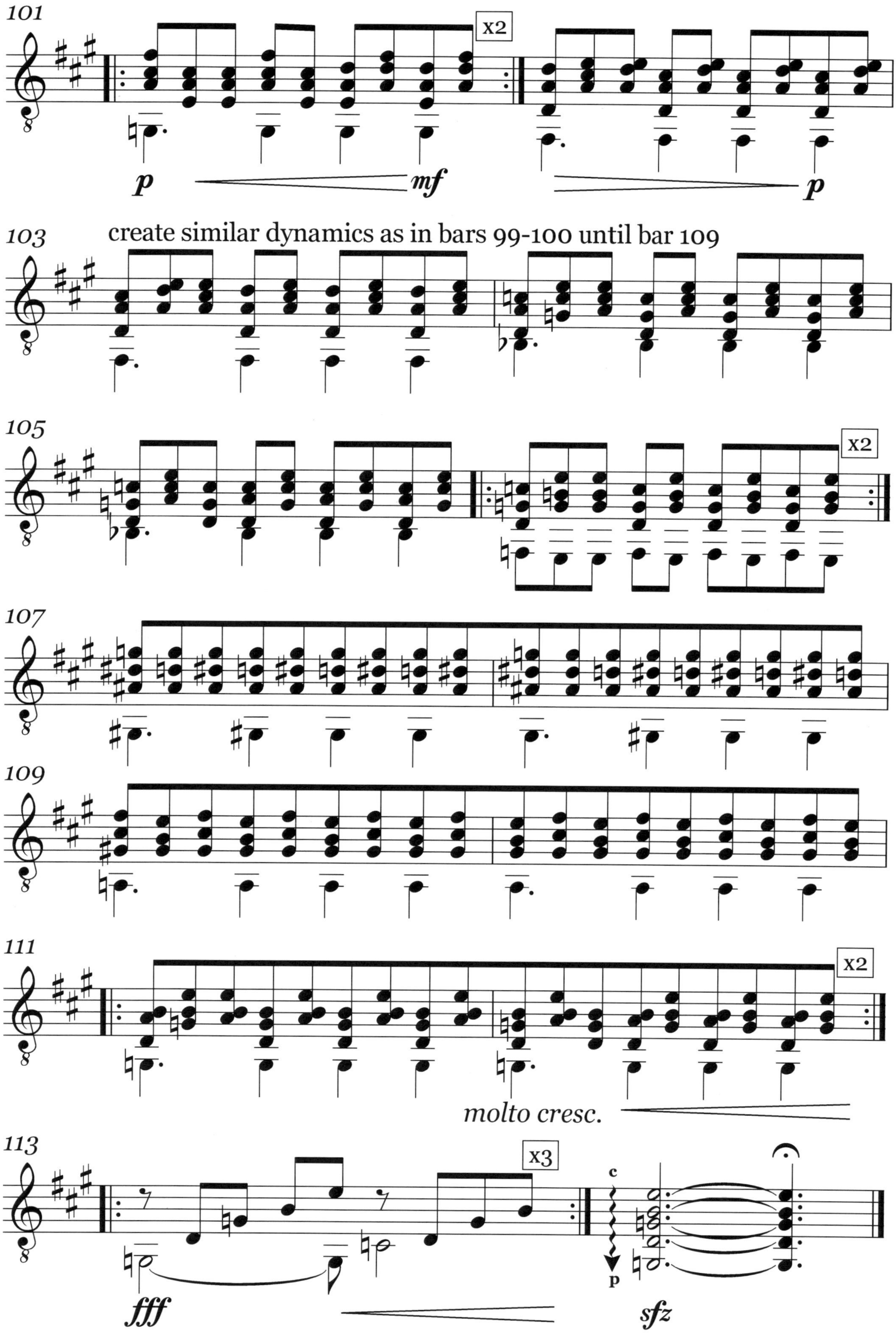
101
x2
p
mf
p
103
create similar dynamics as in bars 99-100 until bar 109
105
x2
107
109
111
x2
molto cresc.
113
x3
c
p
fff
sfz

II
Rainstorm

Dave Flynn
Dublin, March 2000

Freely

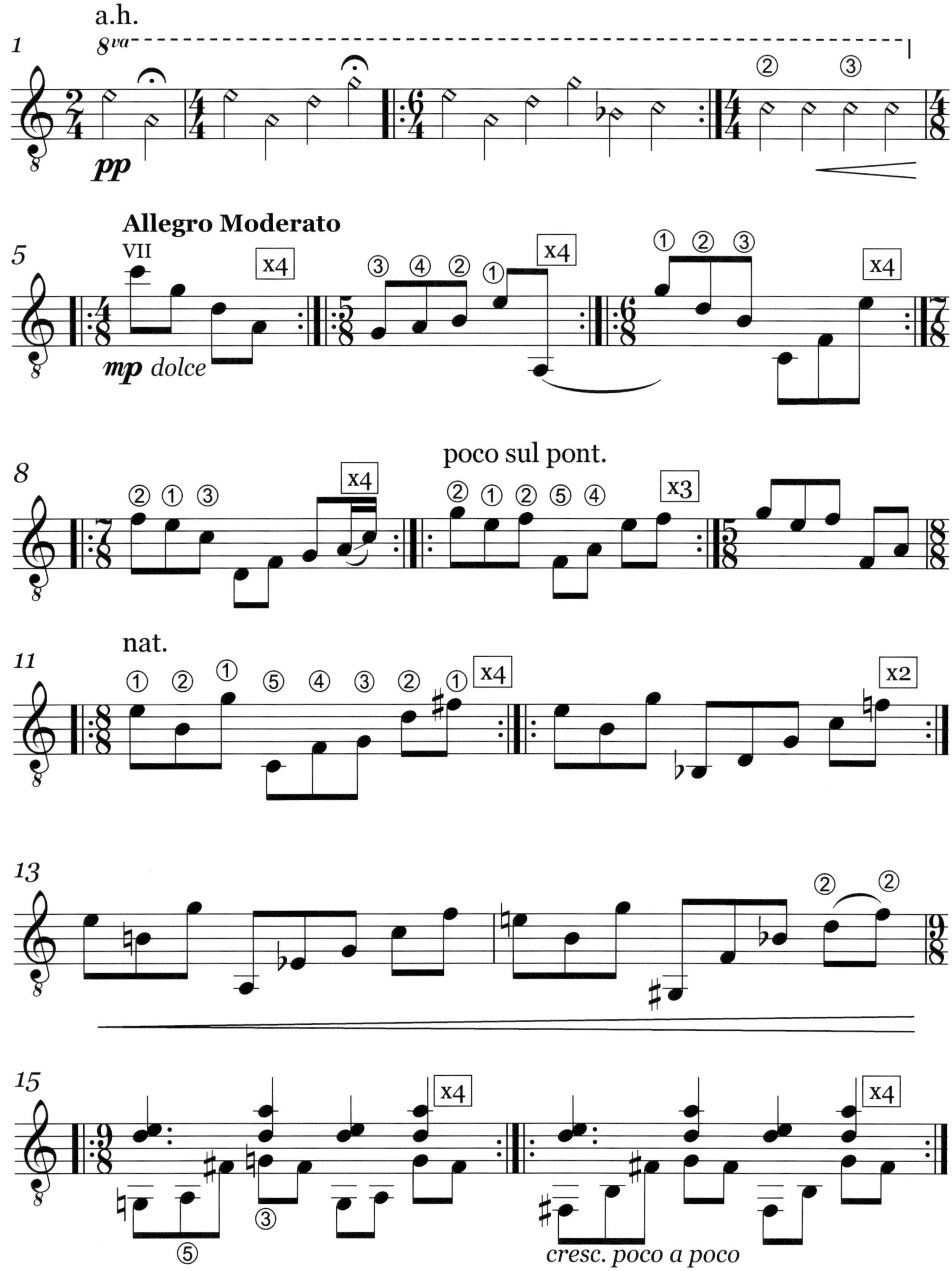

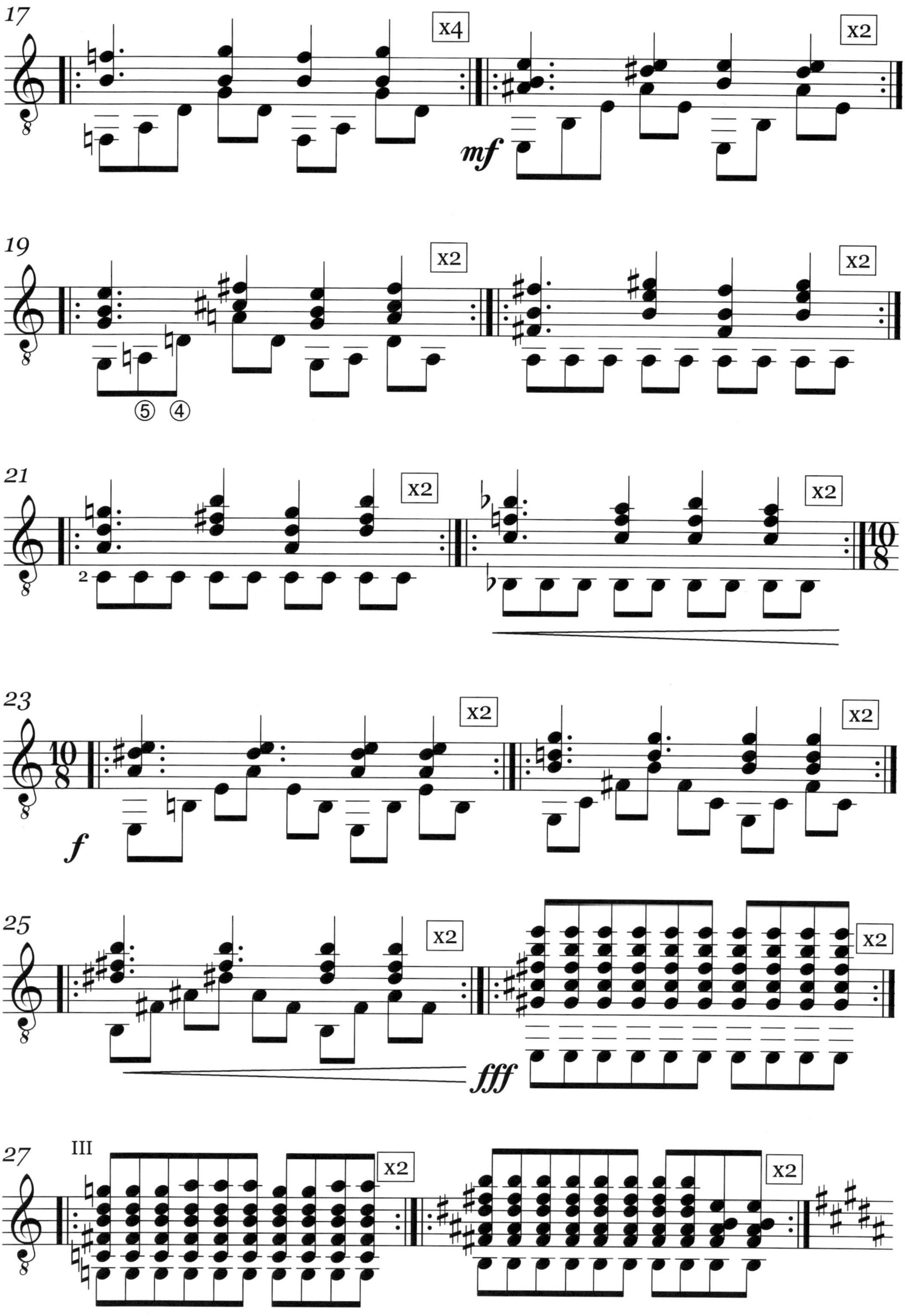
17
x4
x2
mf
19
x2
x2
⑤ ④
21
x2
x2
23
x2
x2
f
25
x2
x2
fff
27
III
x2
x2

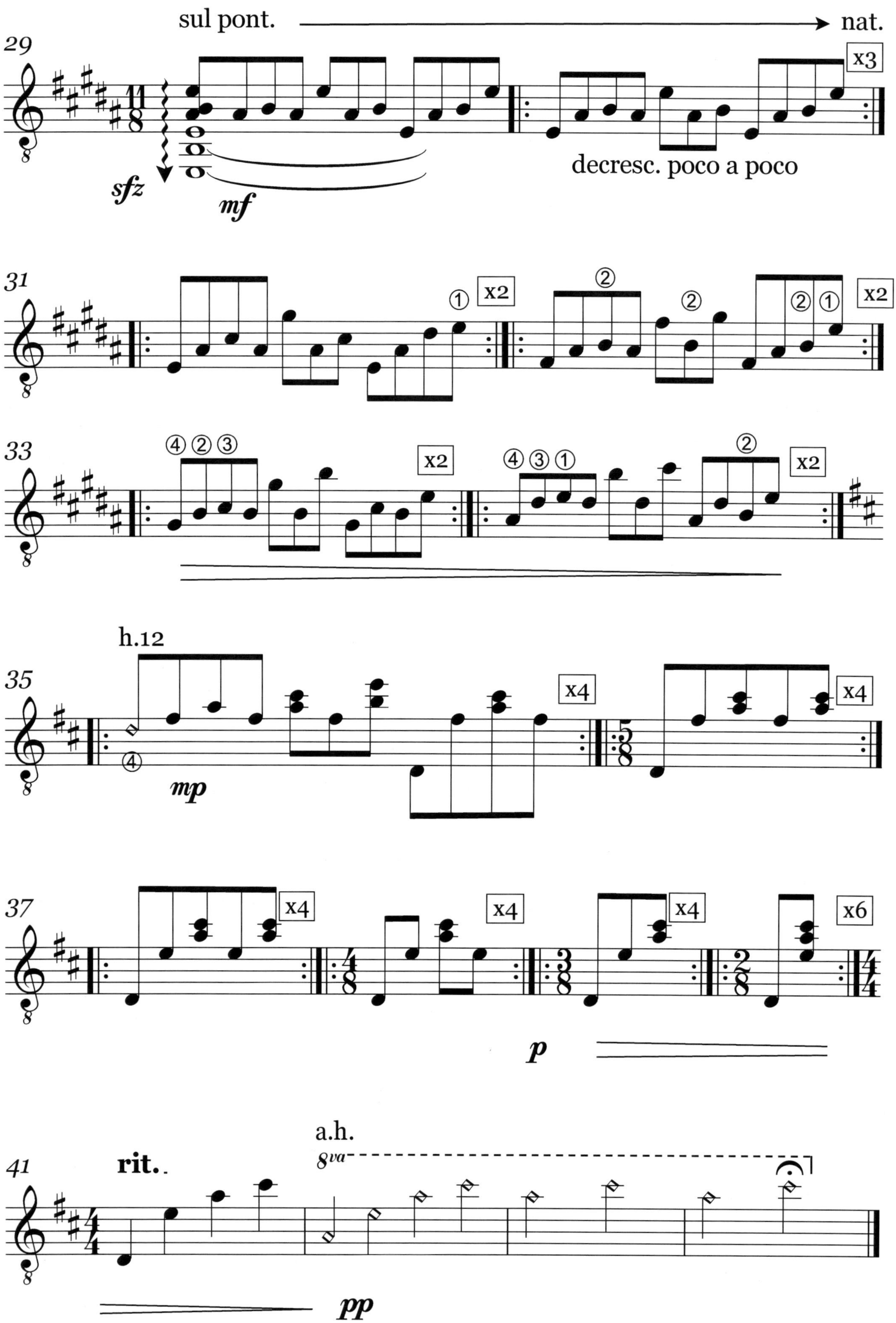
29
sul pont.
nat.
x3
sfz
mf
decresc. poco a poco
31
x2
x2
33
x2
x2
35
h.12
mp
x4
x4
37
x4
x4
x4
x6
p
41
rit.
a.h.
8va
pp

III
Rollercoaster

Allegro Moderato
Let notes ring throughout
with respect to harmonic change

Dave Flynn
Dublin, 1998

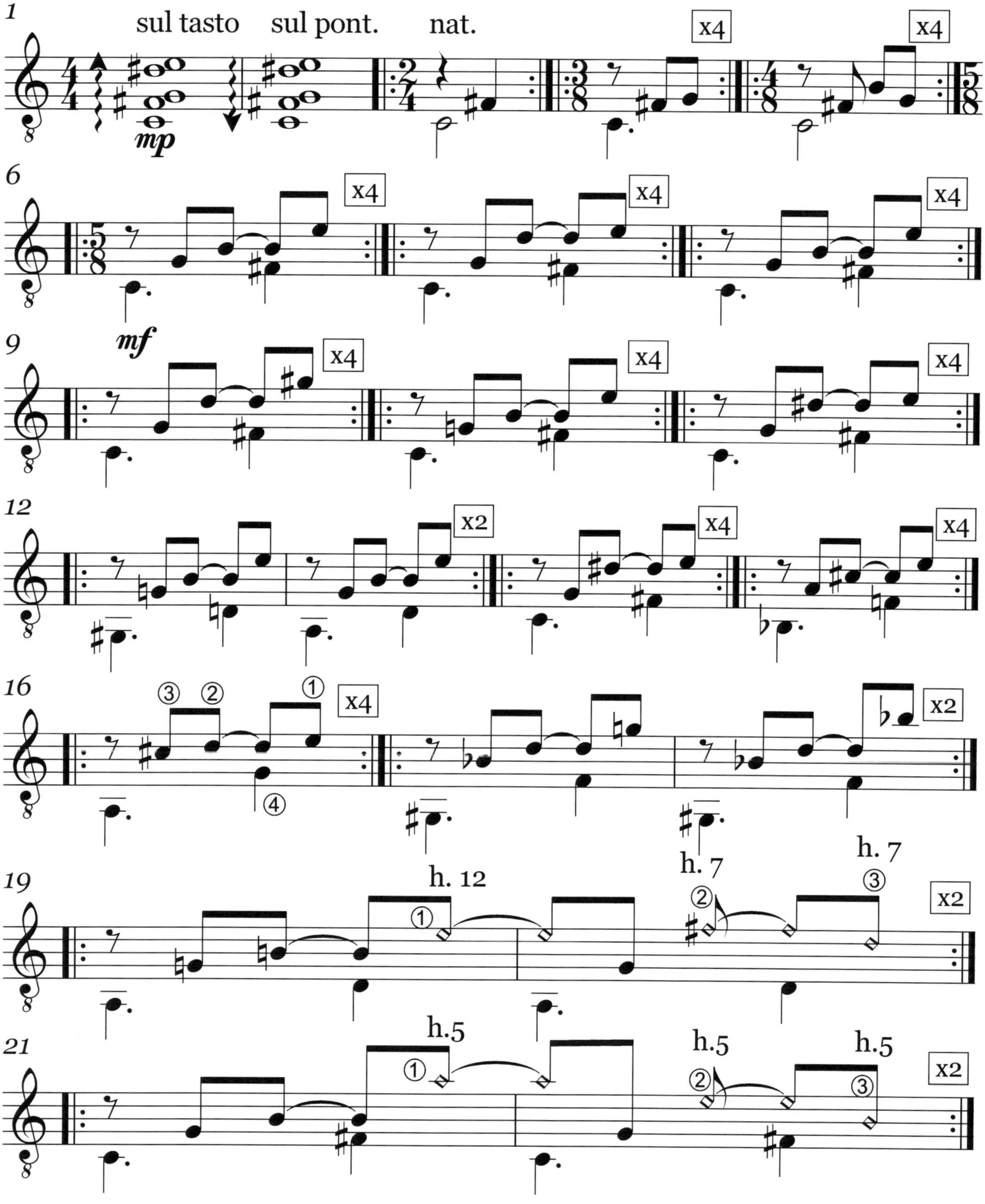

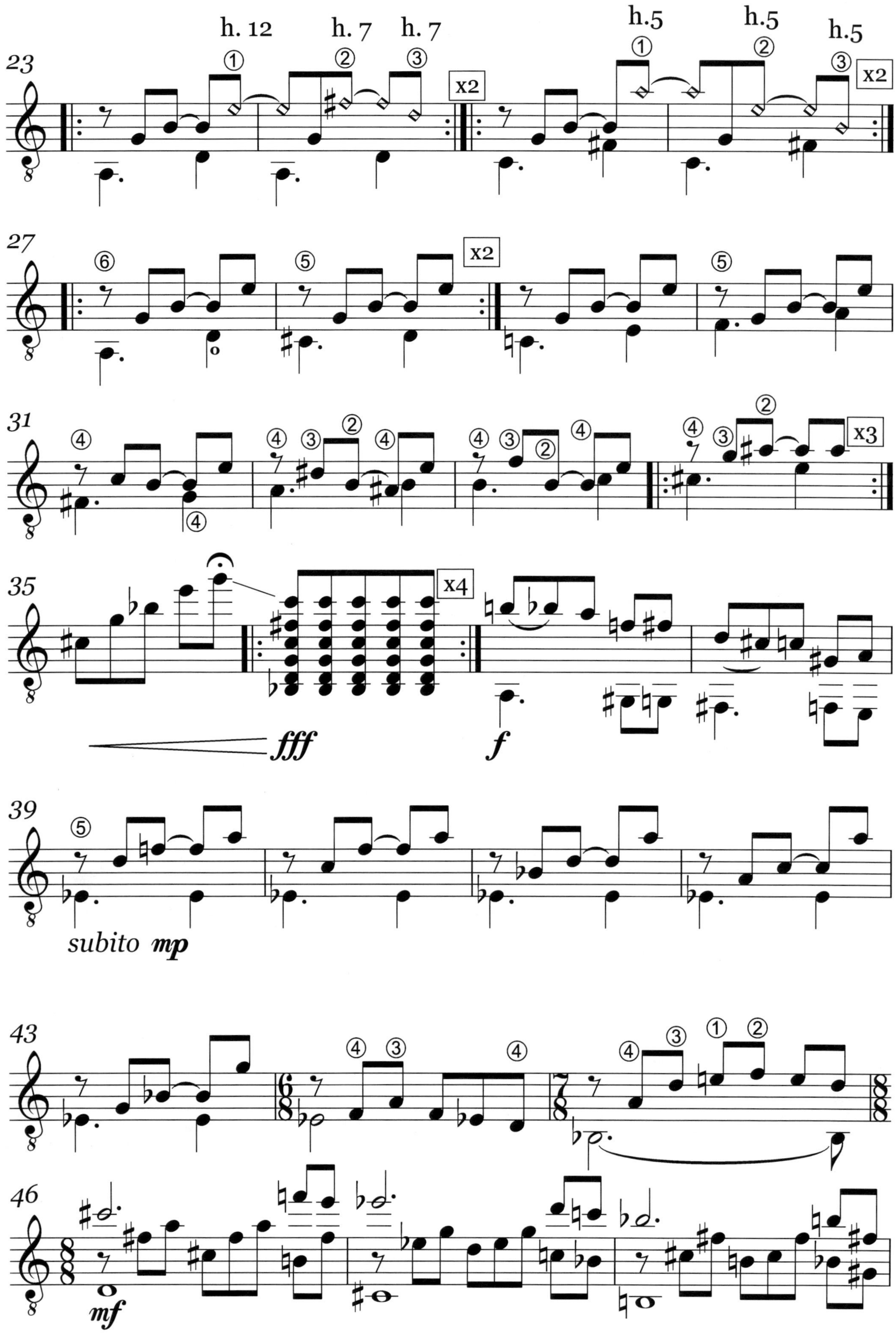
h. 12
h. 7
h. 7
x2
h.5
h.5
h.5
x2
x2
x3
x4
fff
f
subito mp
mf

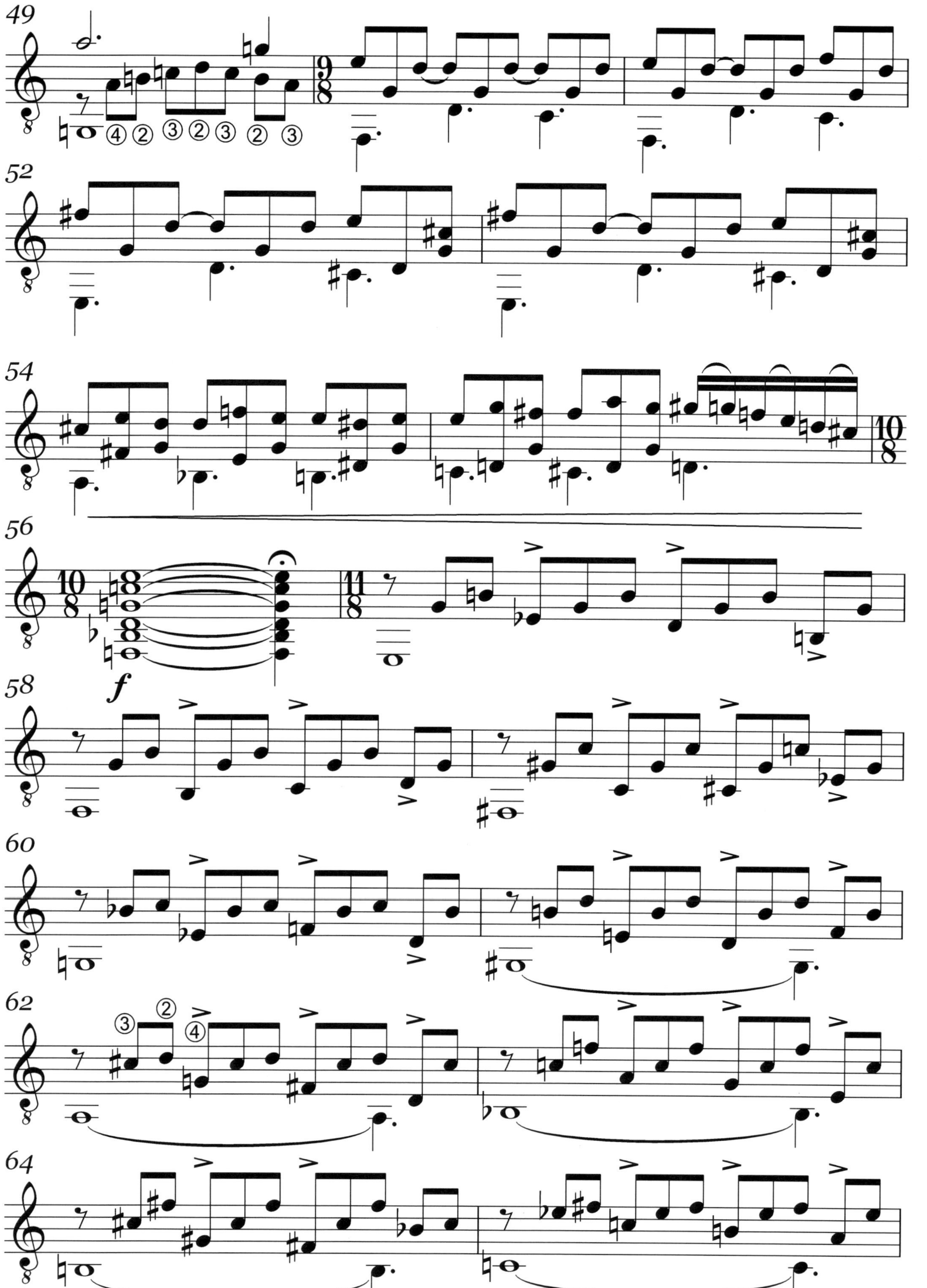
49
52
54
56
58
60
62
64

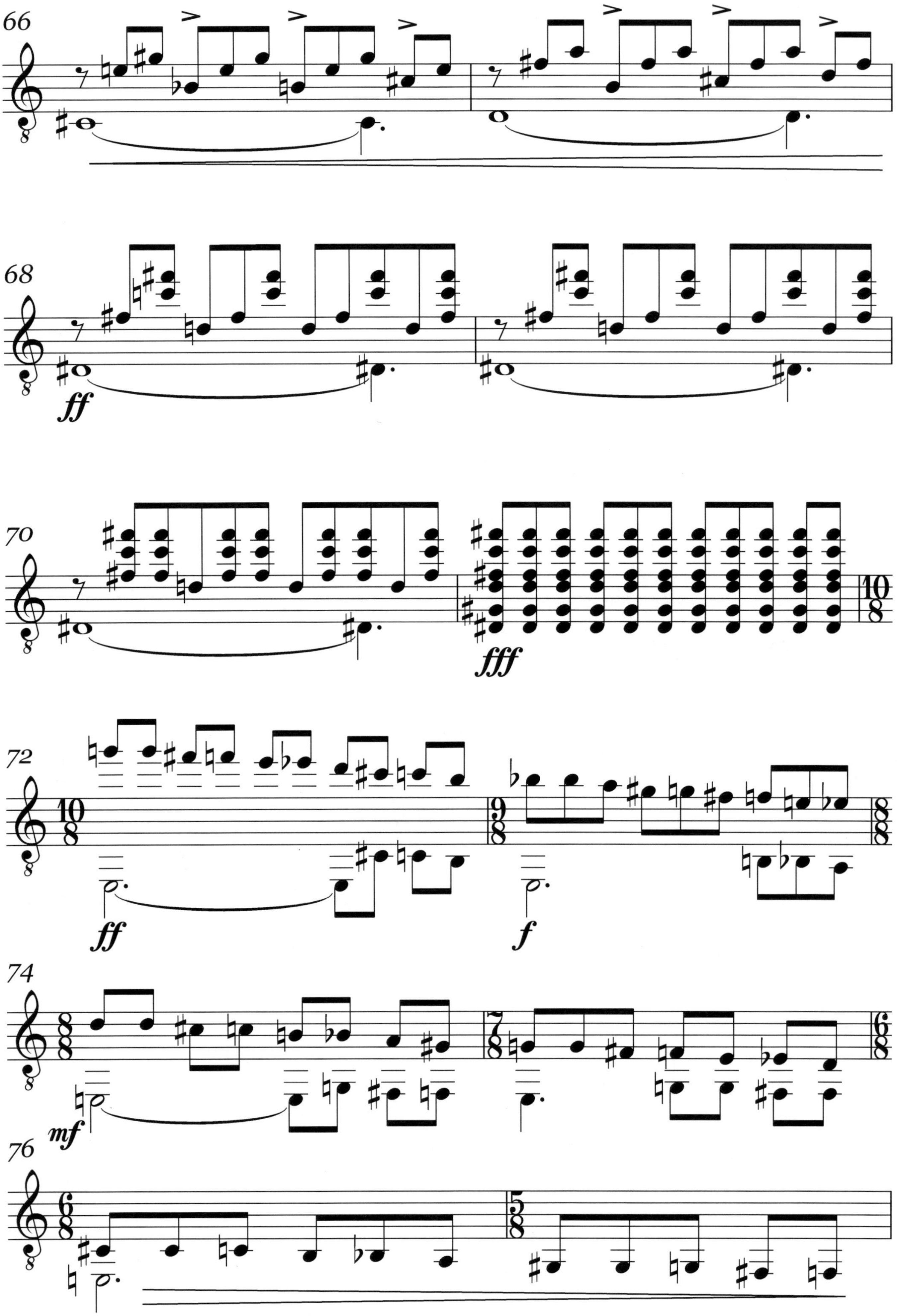
66
68
ff
70
fff
72
ff
f
74
mf
76

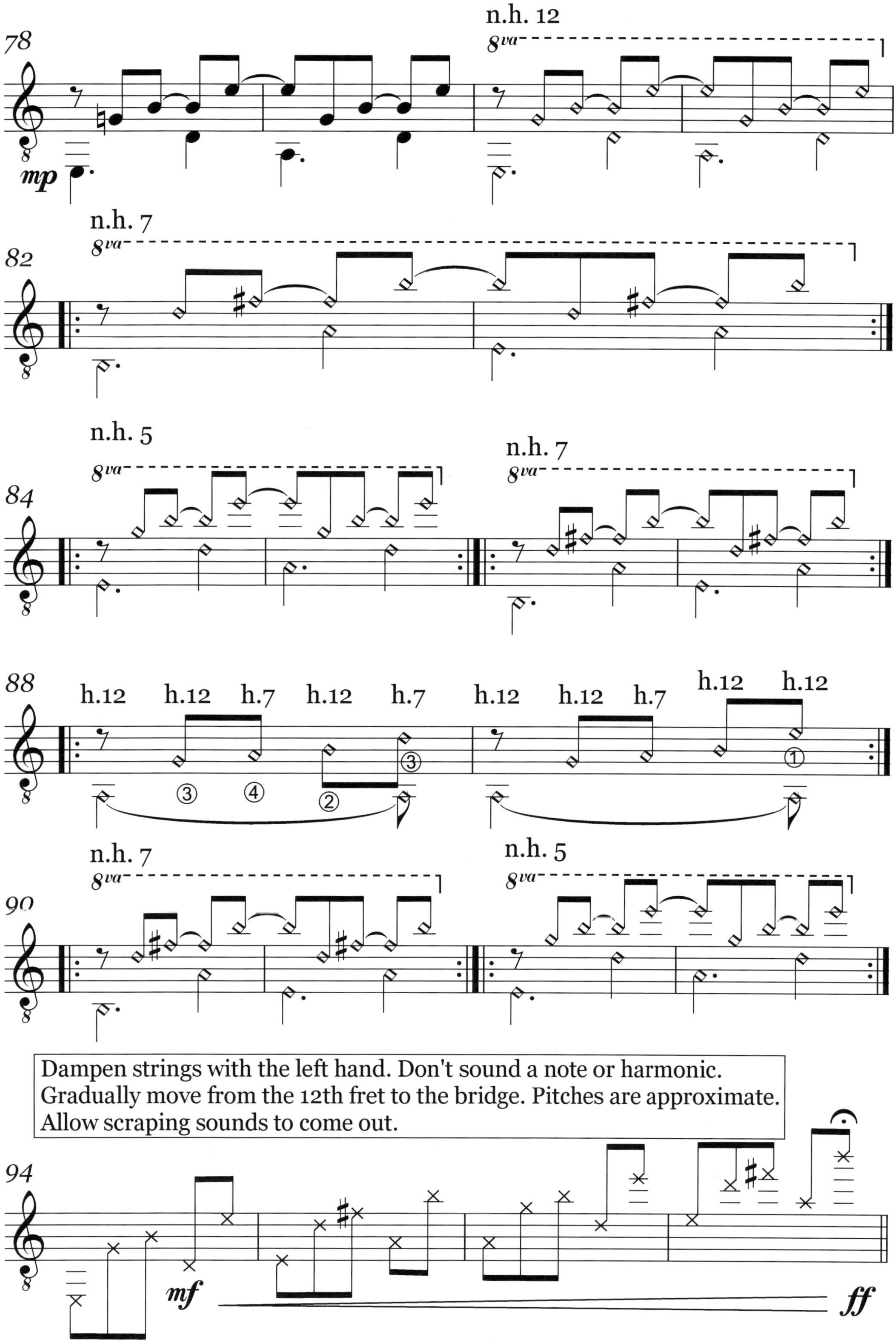
78
n.h. 12
8va
mp
82
n.h. 7
8va
84
n.h. 5
8va
n.h. 7
8va
88
h.12
h.12
h.7
h.12
h.7
h.12
h.12
h.7
h.12
h.12
90
n.h. 7
8va
n.h. 5
8va
Dampen strings with the left hand. Don't sound a note or harmonic.
Gradually move from the 12th fret to the bridge. Pitches are approximate.
Allow scraping sounds to come out.
94
mf
ff

SIX ETUDES FOR FIVE FINGERS (2000-2005)

No.1 Gimme Five
No.2 Homage To Bucko
No.3 The Odd Reel
No.4 Static Slip Jig
No.5 The Glass Harp
No.6 The Glass Abacus

for Charles Postlewate

Six Etudes for Five Fingers

Etude No.1

'Gimme Five'

Dave Flynn
London February 2005

Moderato Molto Rubato

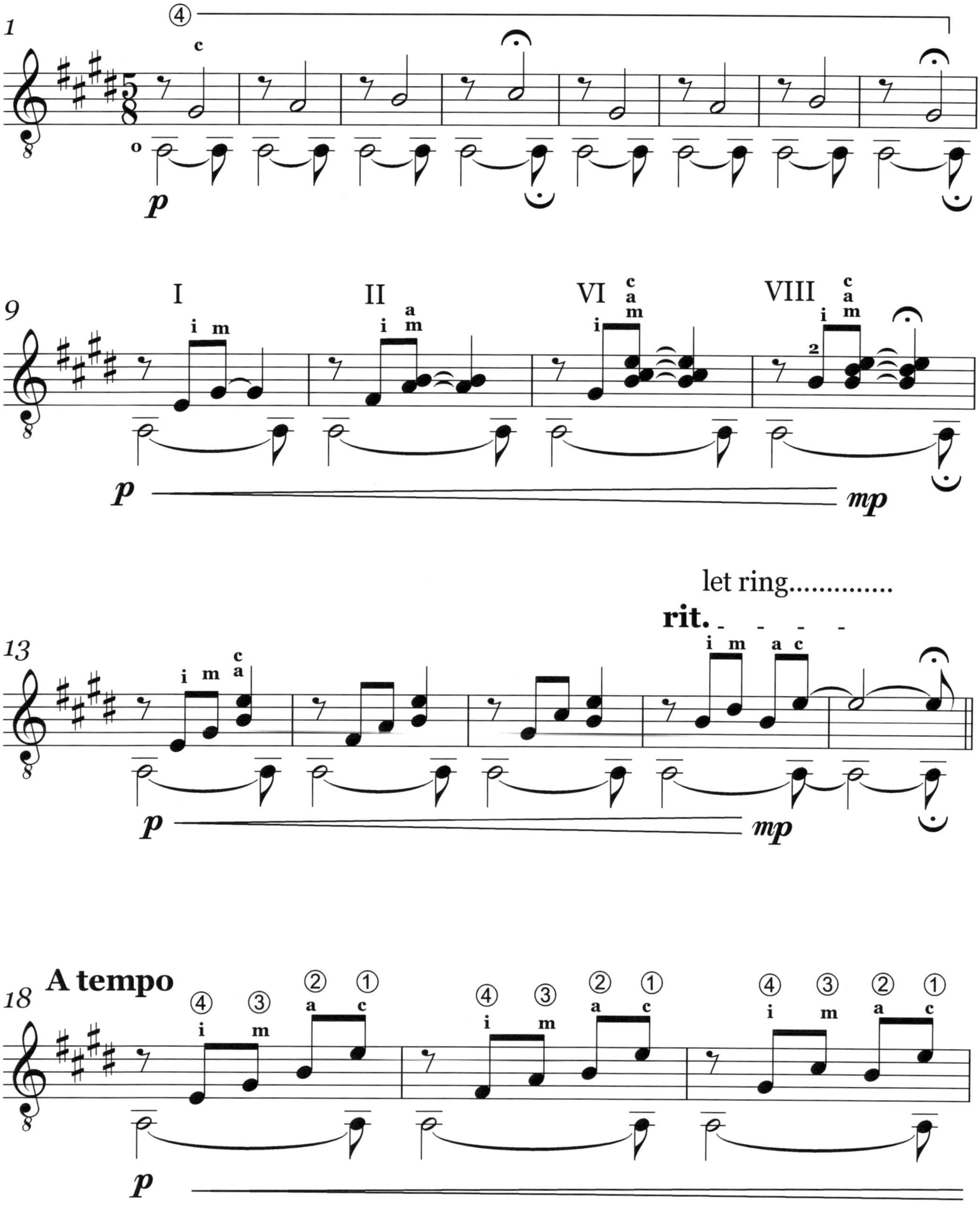

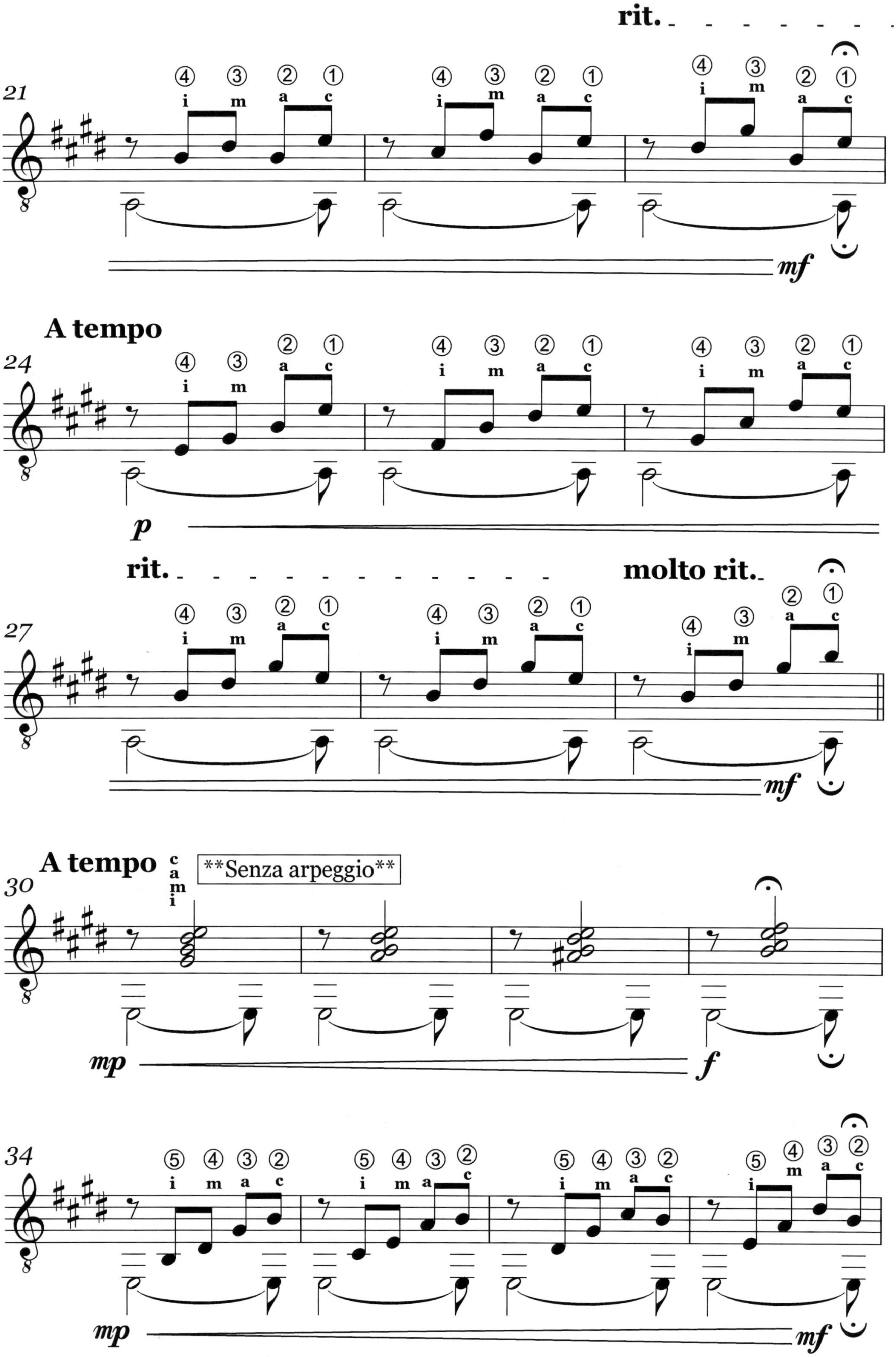
rit.
21
mf
A tempo
24
p
rit.
molto rit.
27
mf
A tempo
Senza arpeggio
30
mp
f
34
mp
mf

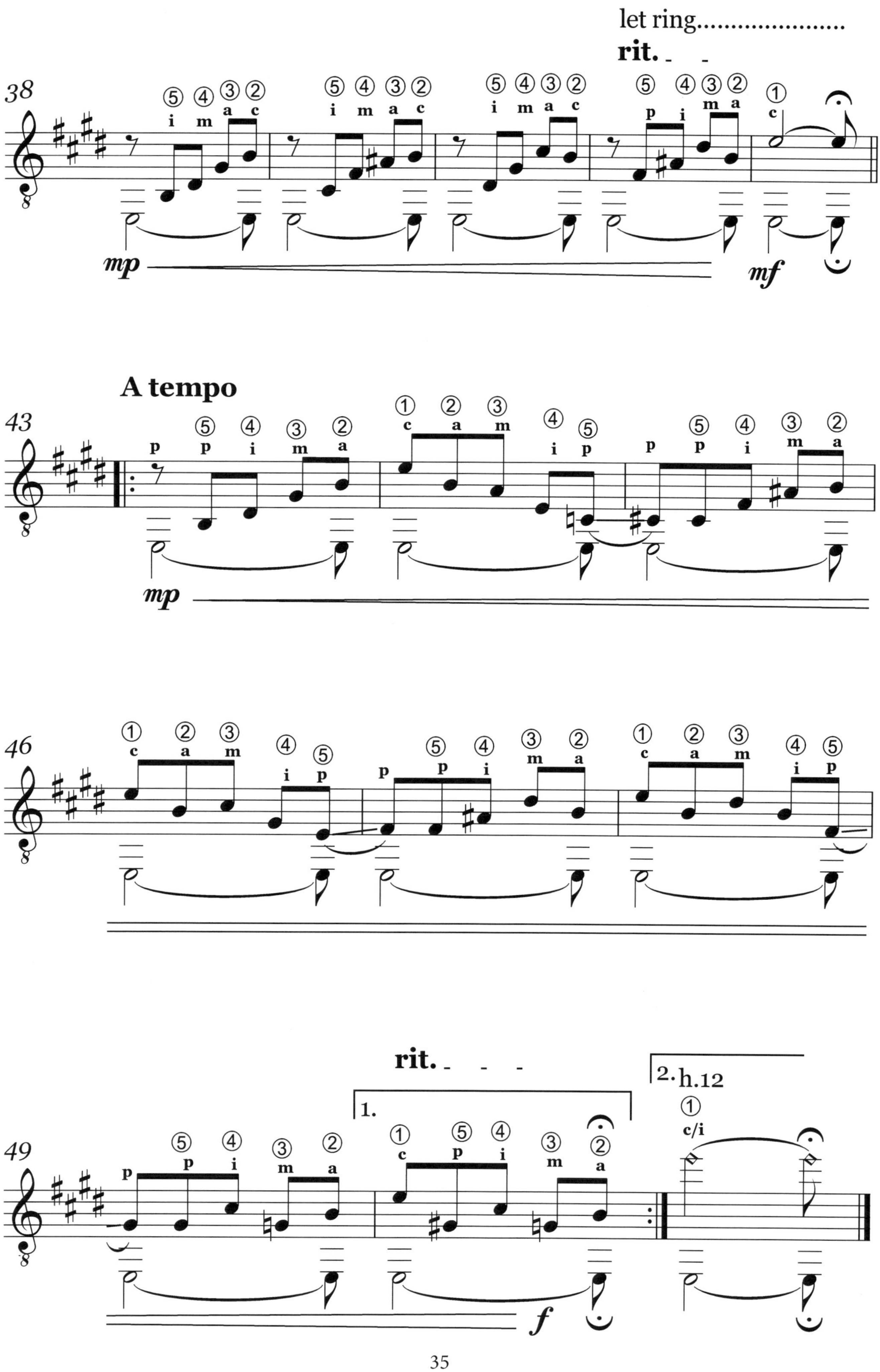
let ring......................
rit.
38
i m a c
i m a c
i m a c
p i m a
c
mp
mf
A tempo
43
p p i m a
c a m
i p
p p i m a
mp
46
c a m
i p
p p i
m a
c a m
i p
rit.
2. h.12
1.
49
p p i m a
c p i m a
c/i
f

for Charles Postlewate

Etude No.2

'Homage To Bucko'

Majestically

Dave Flynn
London, April 2005

♩ = 90-108

♩. = 60-72

Senza arpeggio sempre

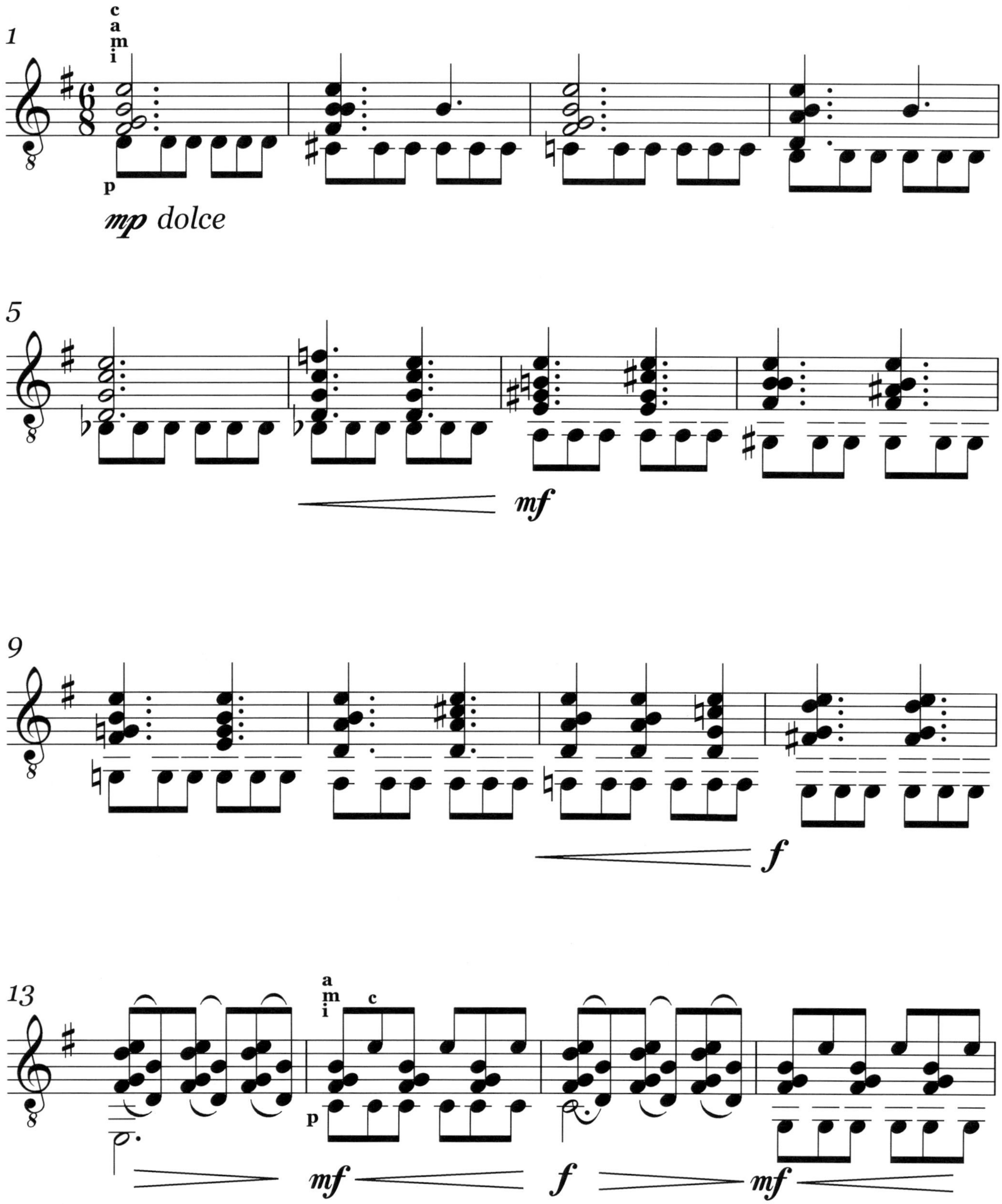

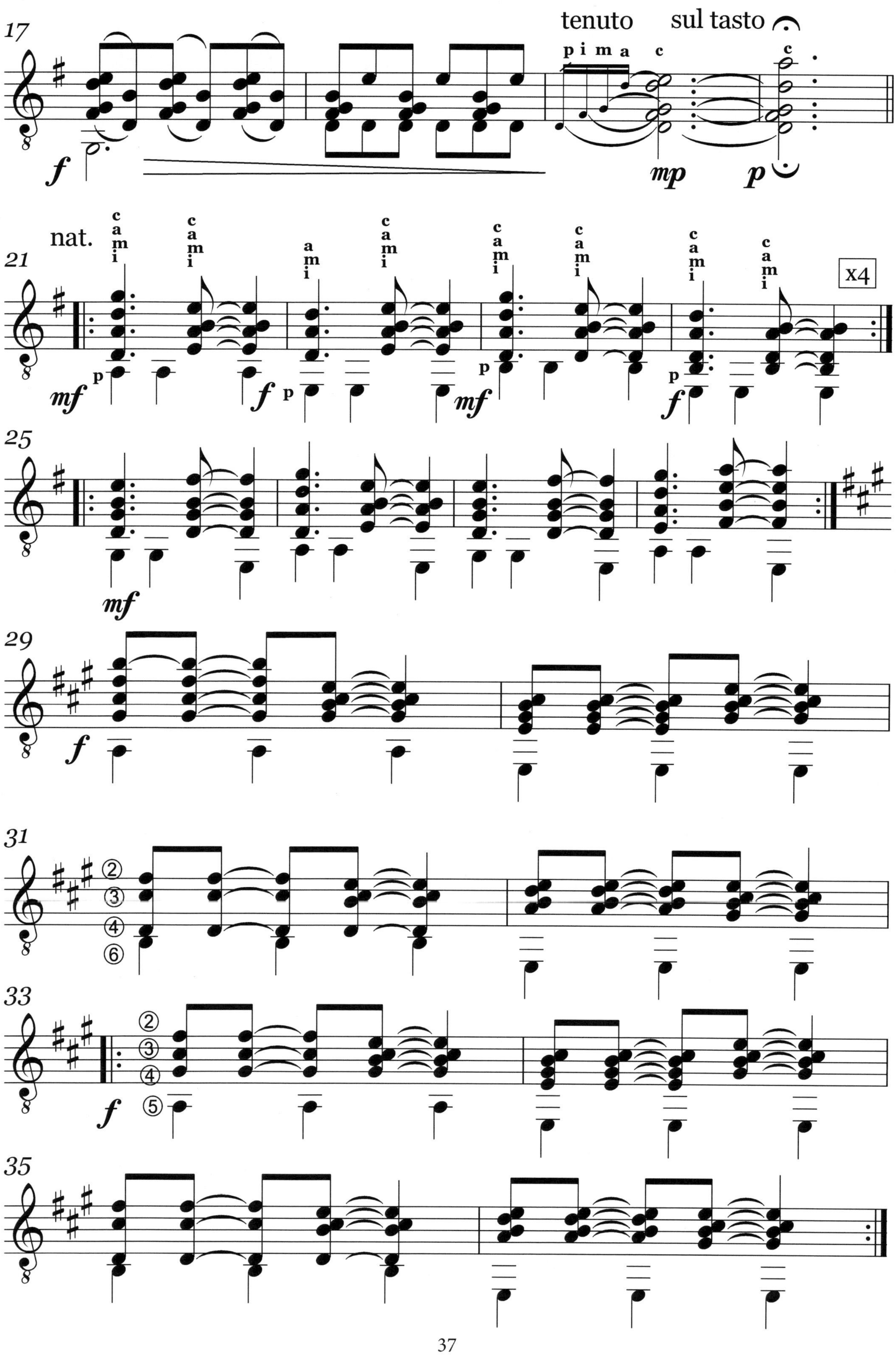
17
tenuto
sul tasto
p i m a
21
nat.
x4
25
29
31
33
35

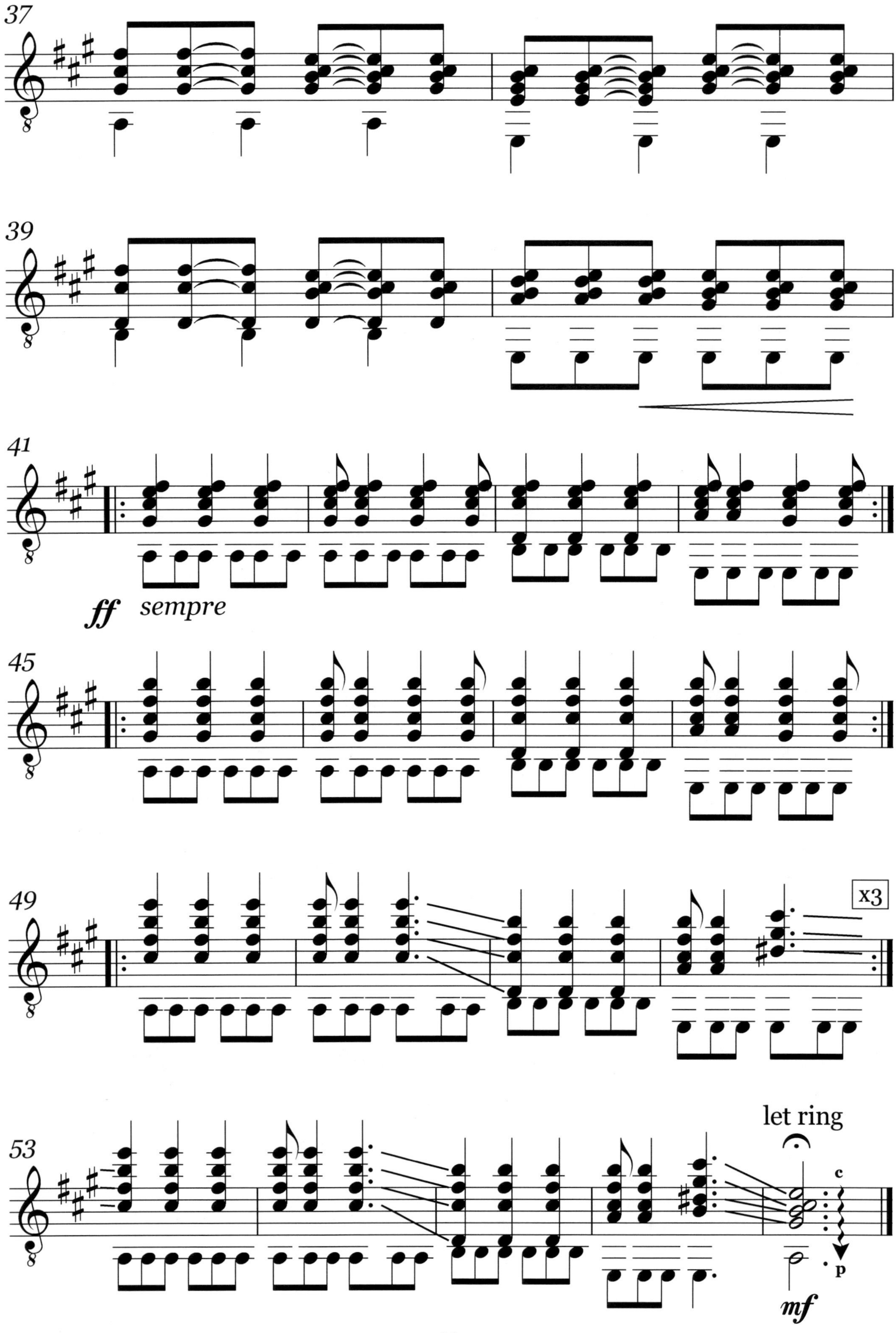
ff sempre
x3
let ring
c
p
mf

for Charles Postlewate

Etude No.3

'The Odd Reel'

With an Irish lilt

♩ = 96

or ♩ = 126 Tempo may be either

Dave Flynn
London, March 2005

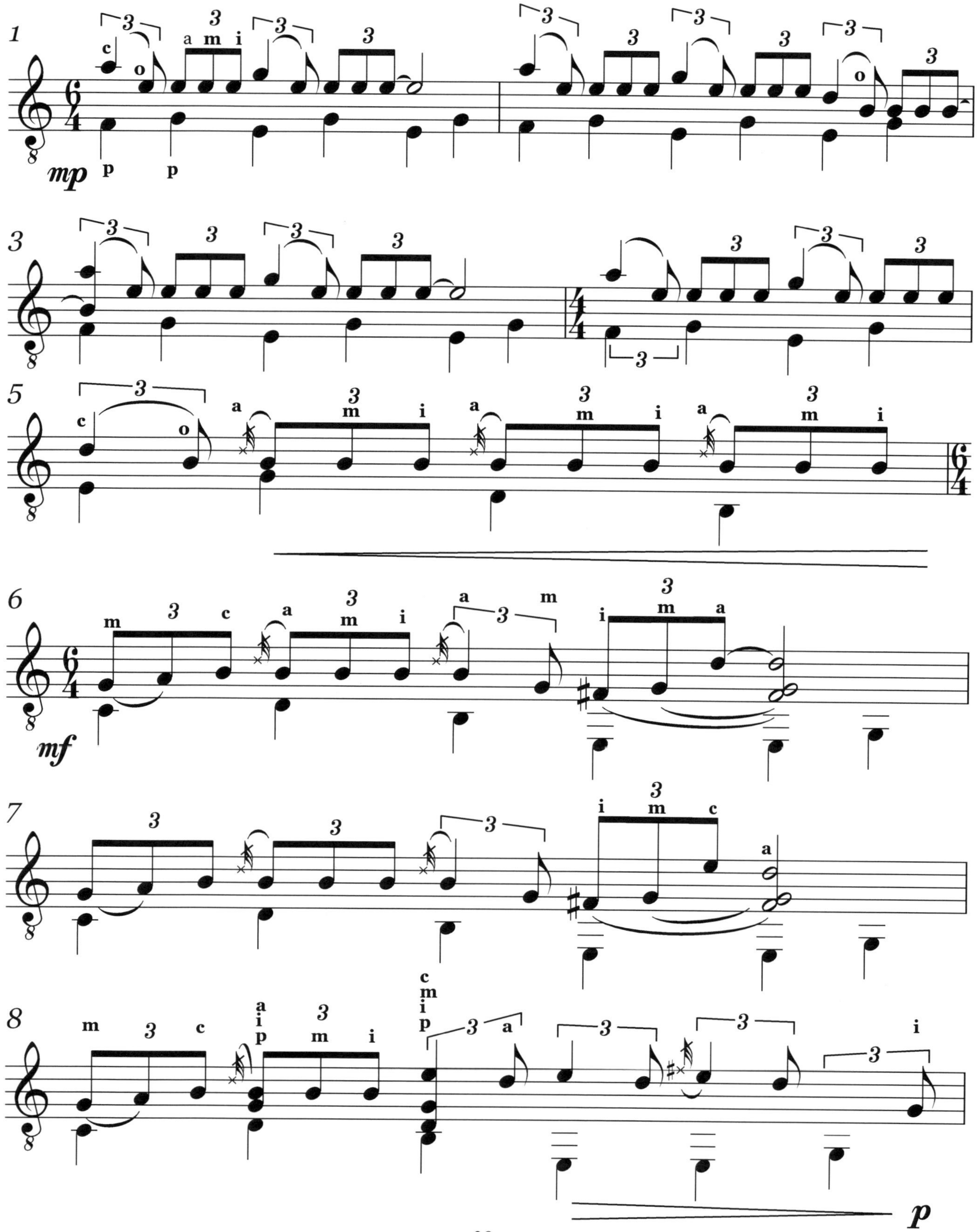

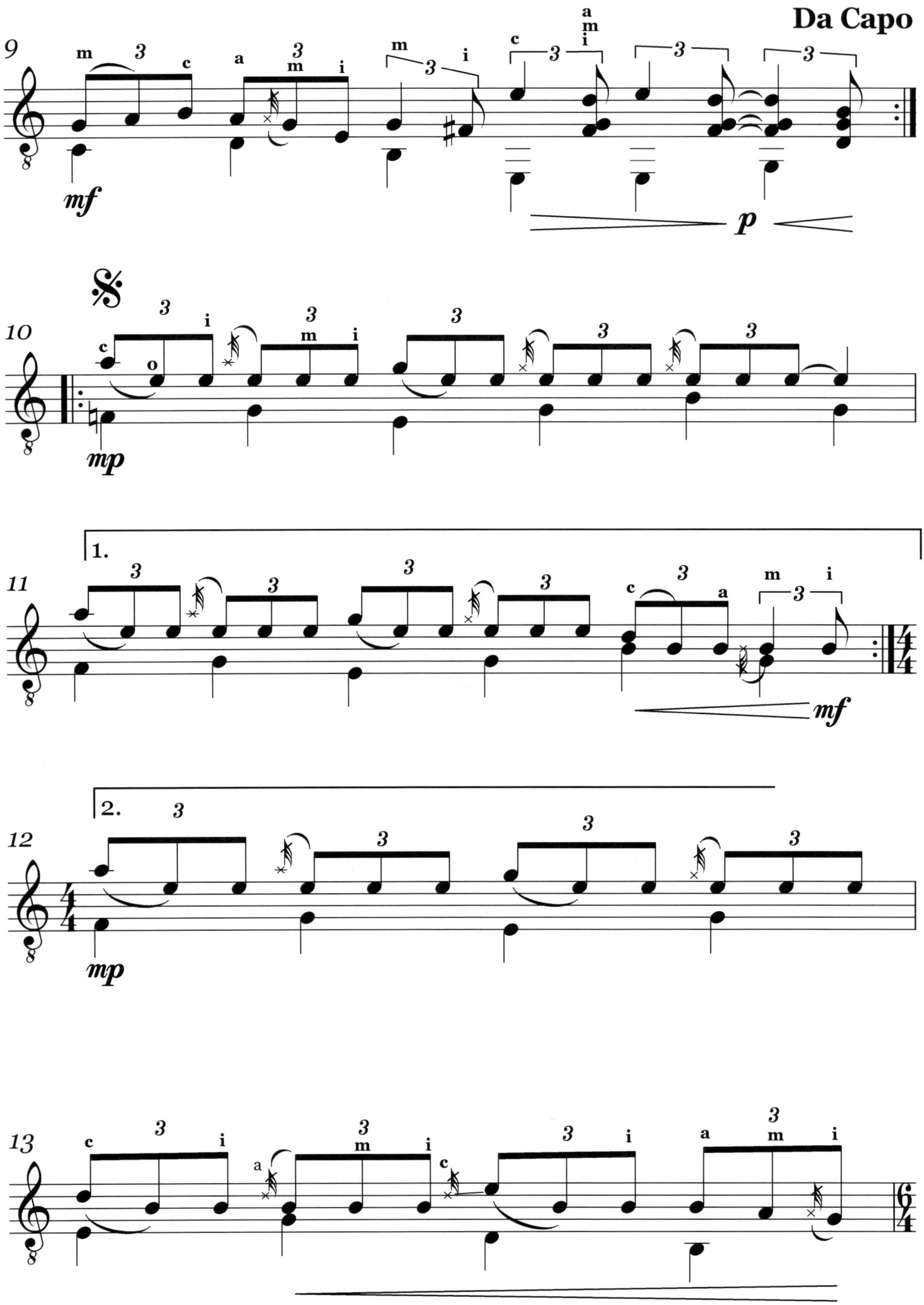
Da Capo

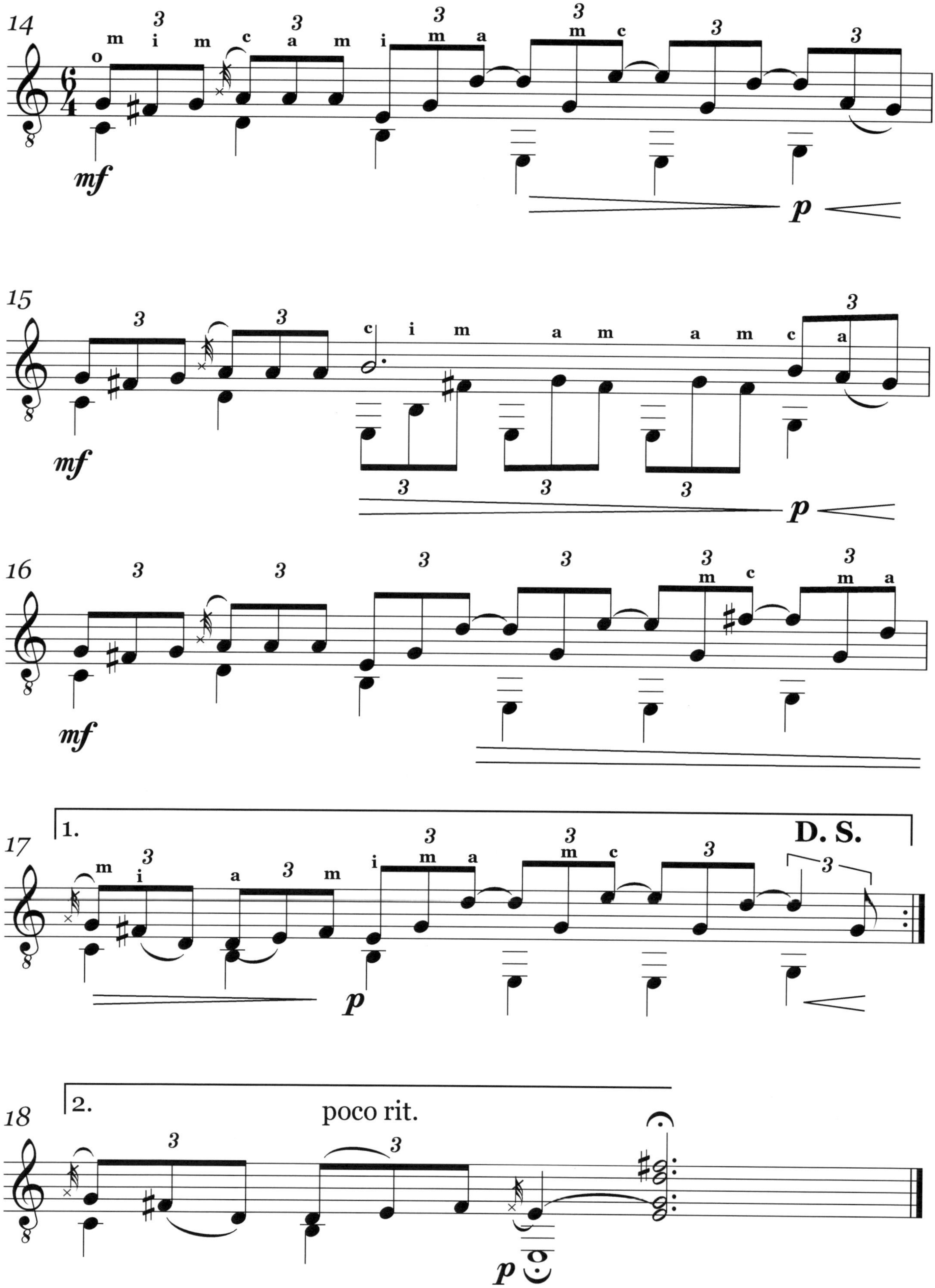
14
mf
p
15
mf
p
16
mf
17
1.
D. S.
p
18
2.
poco rit.
p

for Charles Postlewate

Etude No.4

'Static Slip Jig'

Dave Flynn
London March 2005

In the style of an Irish Slip Jig

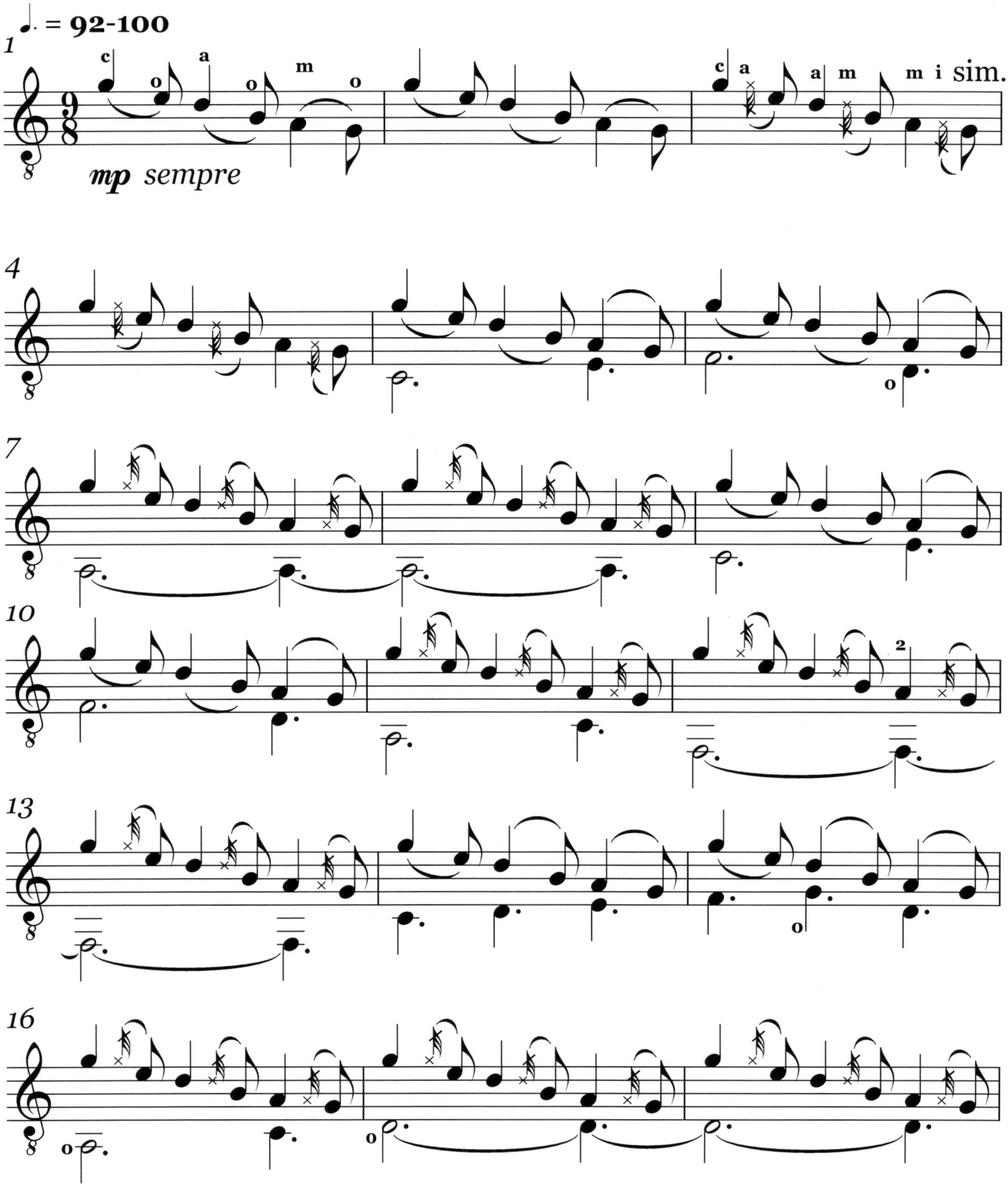

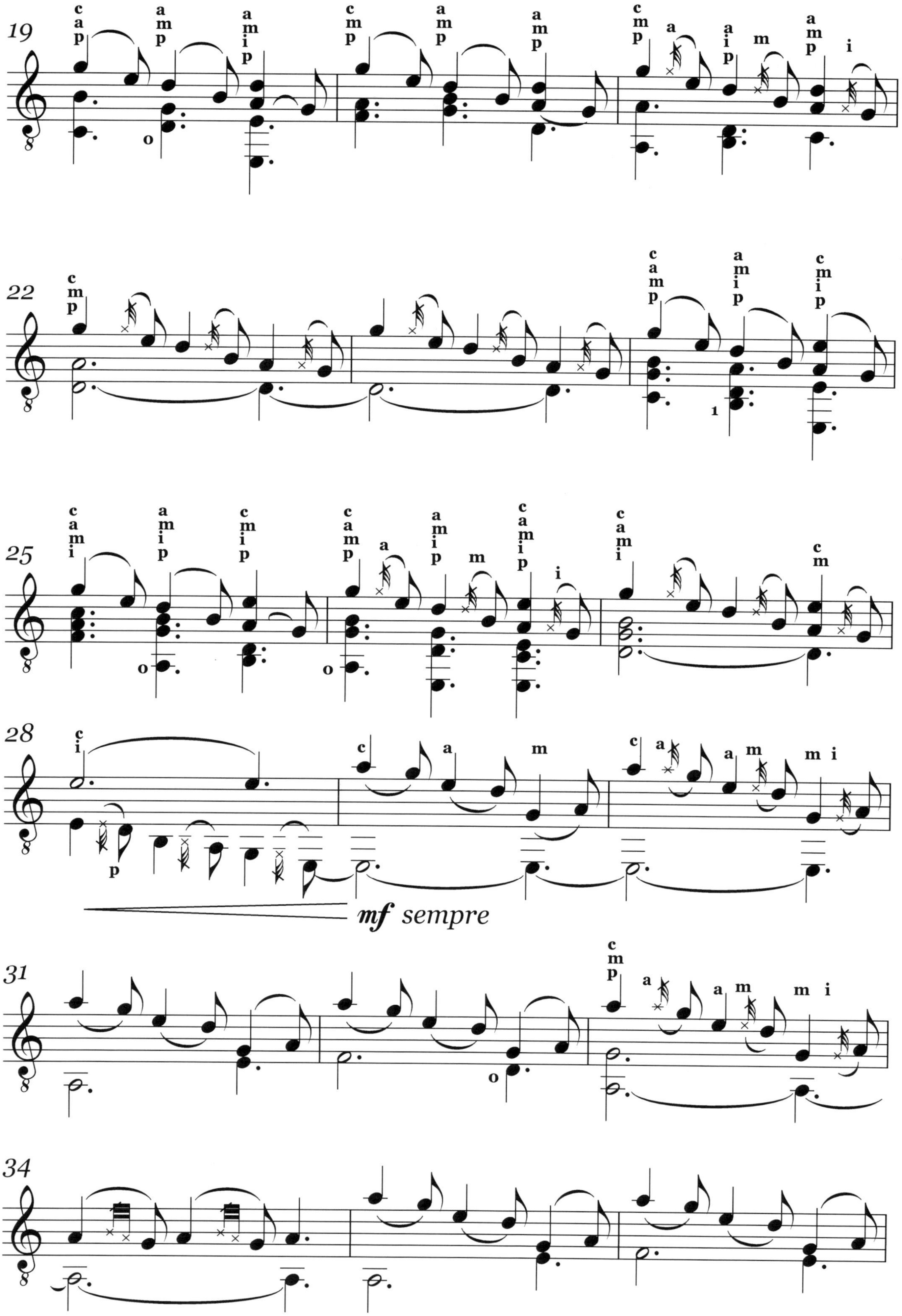
19
22
25
28
mf sempre
31
34

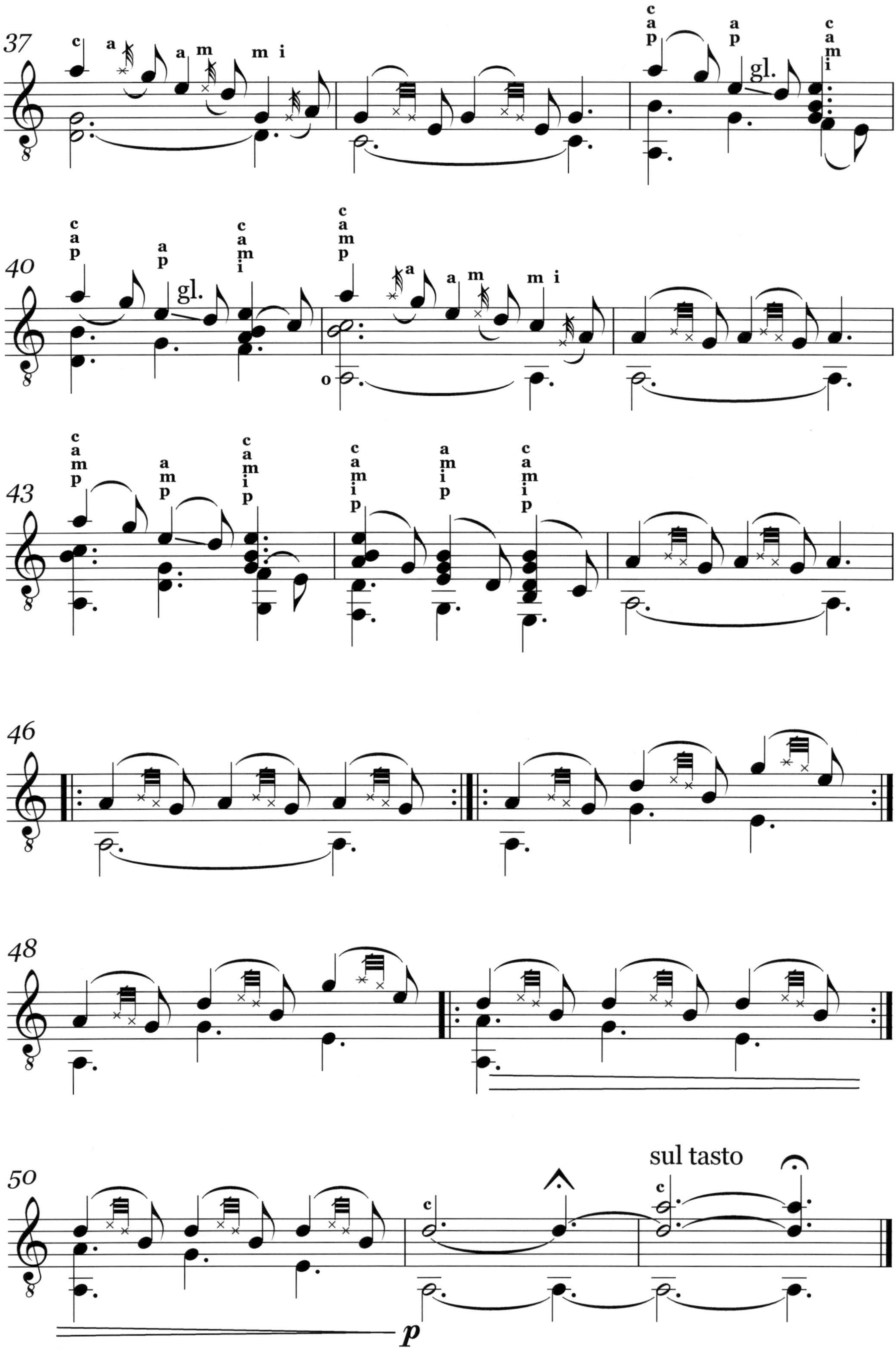
37
c a a m m i
c a p
a p
gl.
c a m i
40
c a p
a p
gl.
c a m i
c a m p
a a m m i
o
43
c a m p
a m p
c a m i p
c a m i p
a m i p
c a m i p
46
48
50
c
sul tasto
c
p

This page has been left blank to avoid an awkward page turn.

In honour of Philip Glass

Etude No.5

The Glass Harp

Dave Flynn
(2000, rediscovered and revised 2011)

All sections with repeat marks should be varied in the number of repeats played. Shorter sections should be repeated 3-6 times, longer sections no more than 3. For example, I usually play bars 1-4 four times each and bars 27-28 twice each. Tempo and dynamics are up to the performer, but use the same tempo throughout

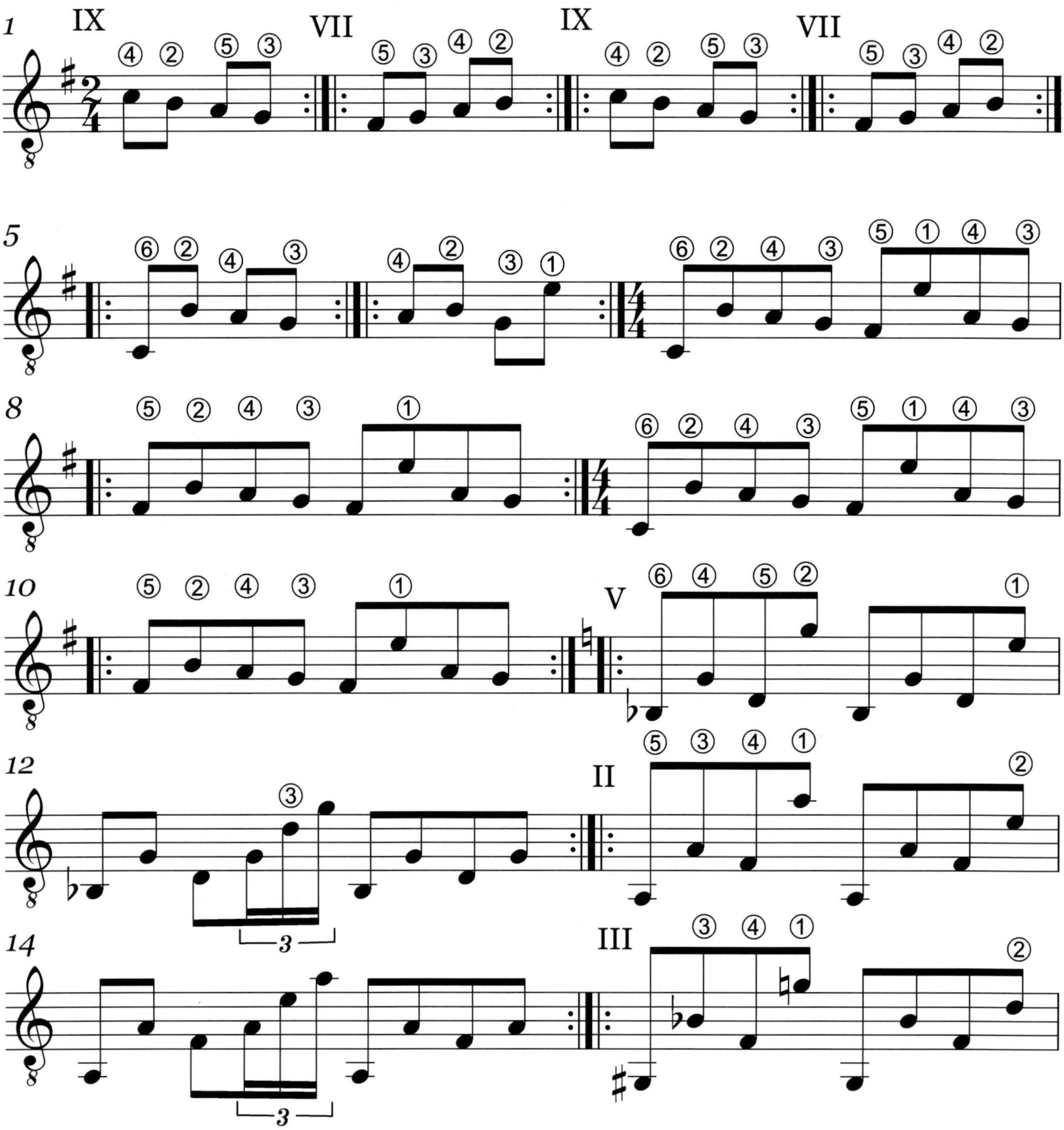

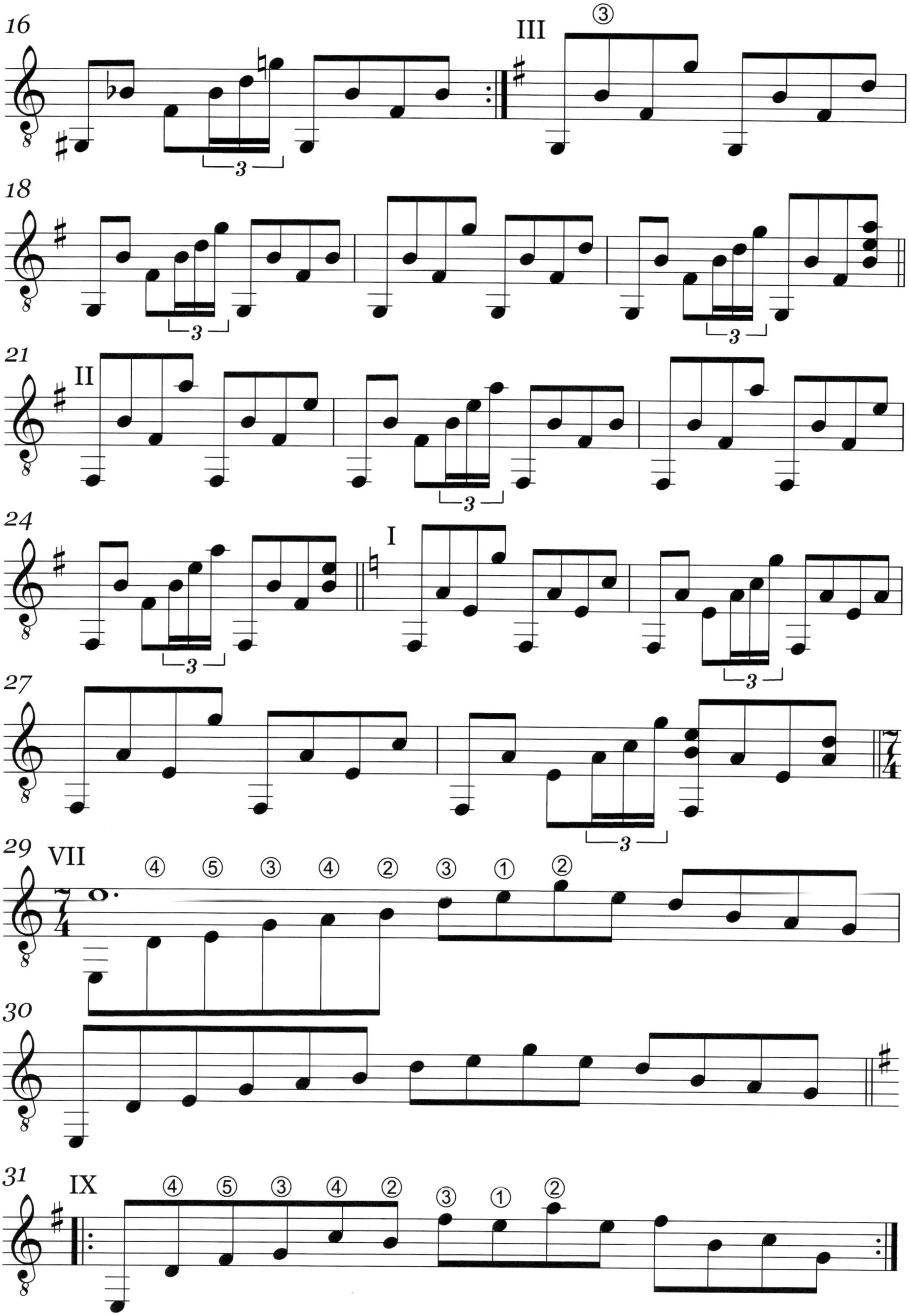
16
III
③
18
21
II
24
I
27
29
VII
④ ⑤ ③ ④ ② ③ ① ②
30
31
IX
④ ⑤ ③ ④ ② ③ ① ②

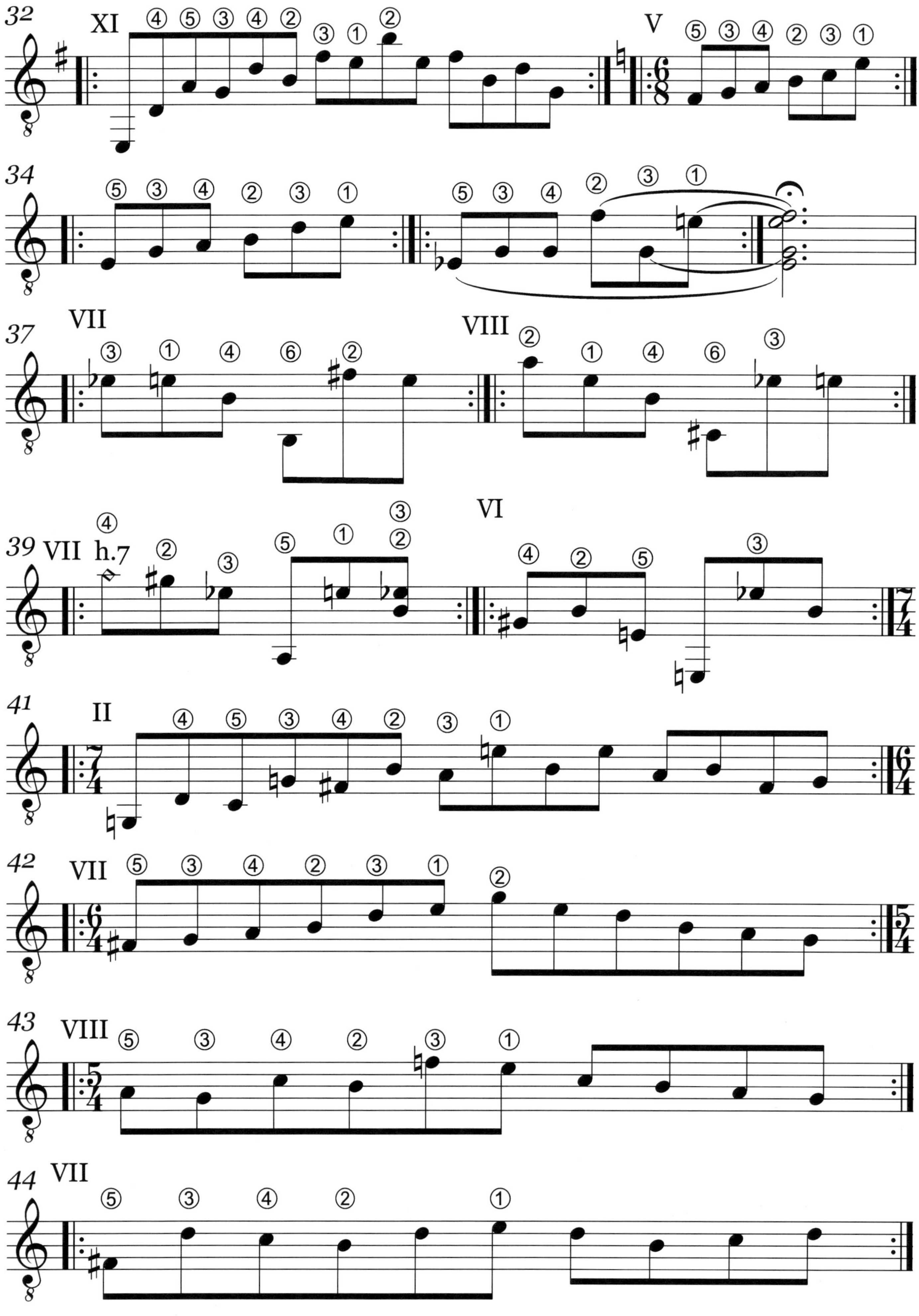
32
XI
V
34
37
VII
VIII
39
VII
h.7
VI
41
II
42
VII
43
VIII
44
VII

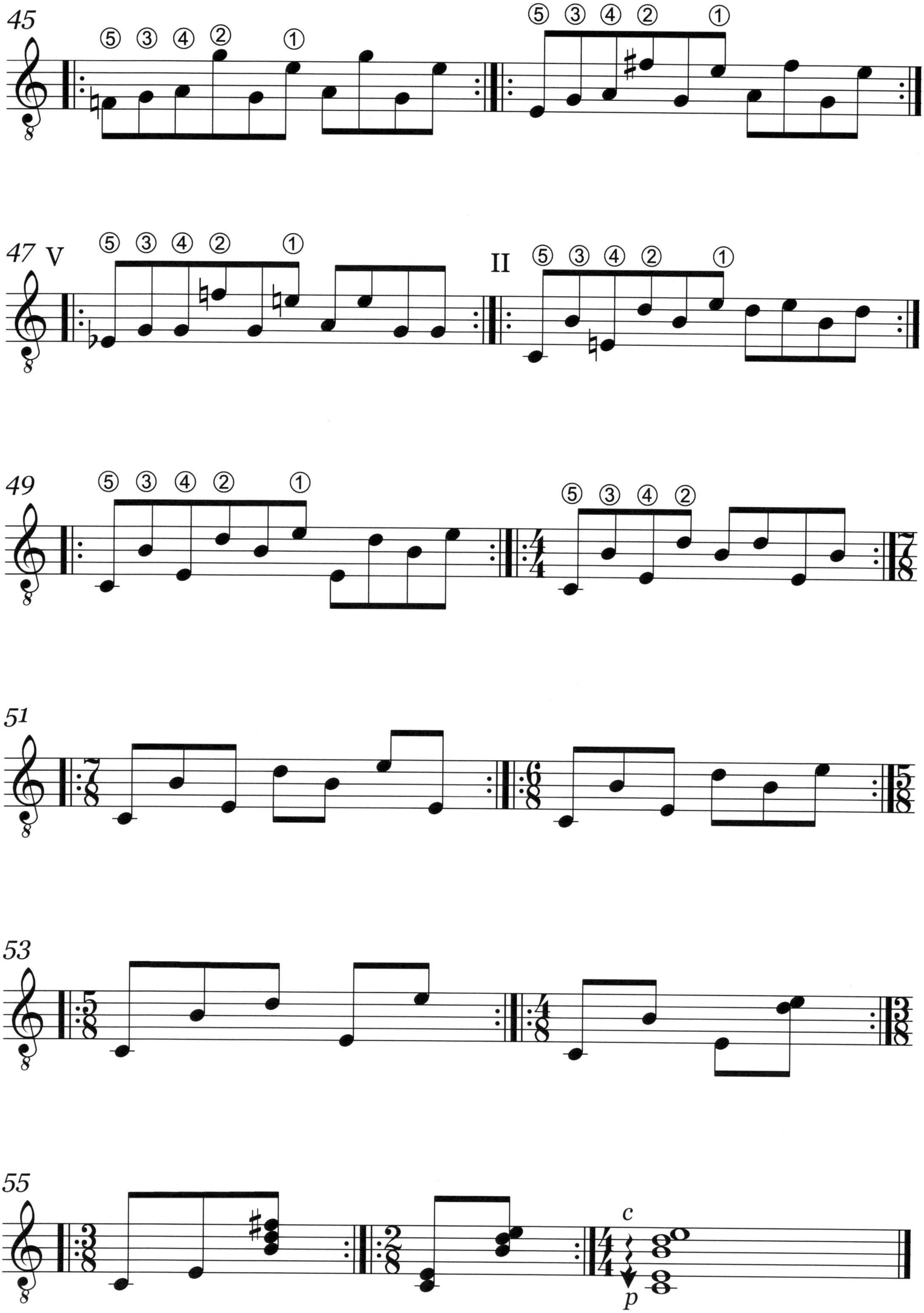
45
⑤ ③ ④ ② ①
⑤ ③ ④ ② ①
47 V
⑤ ③ ④ ② ①
II
⑤ ③ ④ ② ①
49
⑤ ③ ④ ② ①
⑤ ③ ④ ②
51
53
55
c
p

Etude No.6

The Glass Abacus

Dave Flynn
(2000/Rediscovered and Revised 2011)

All sections with repeat marks should be varied in the number of repeats played. Shorter sections should be repeated 3-6 times, longer sections no more than 3. Choose your own dynamics, timbral changes and tempo. Stick to one solid tempo throughout.

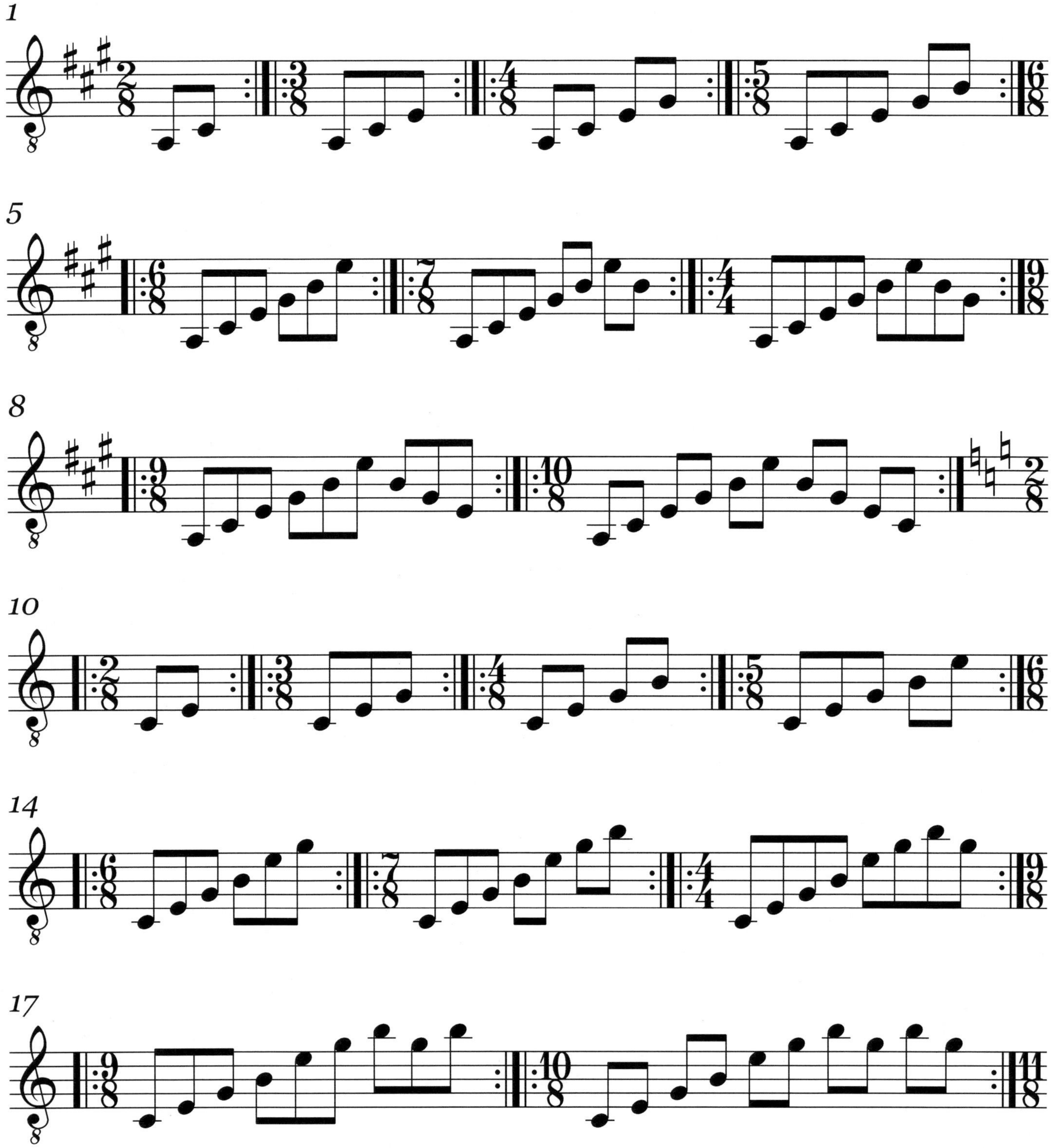

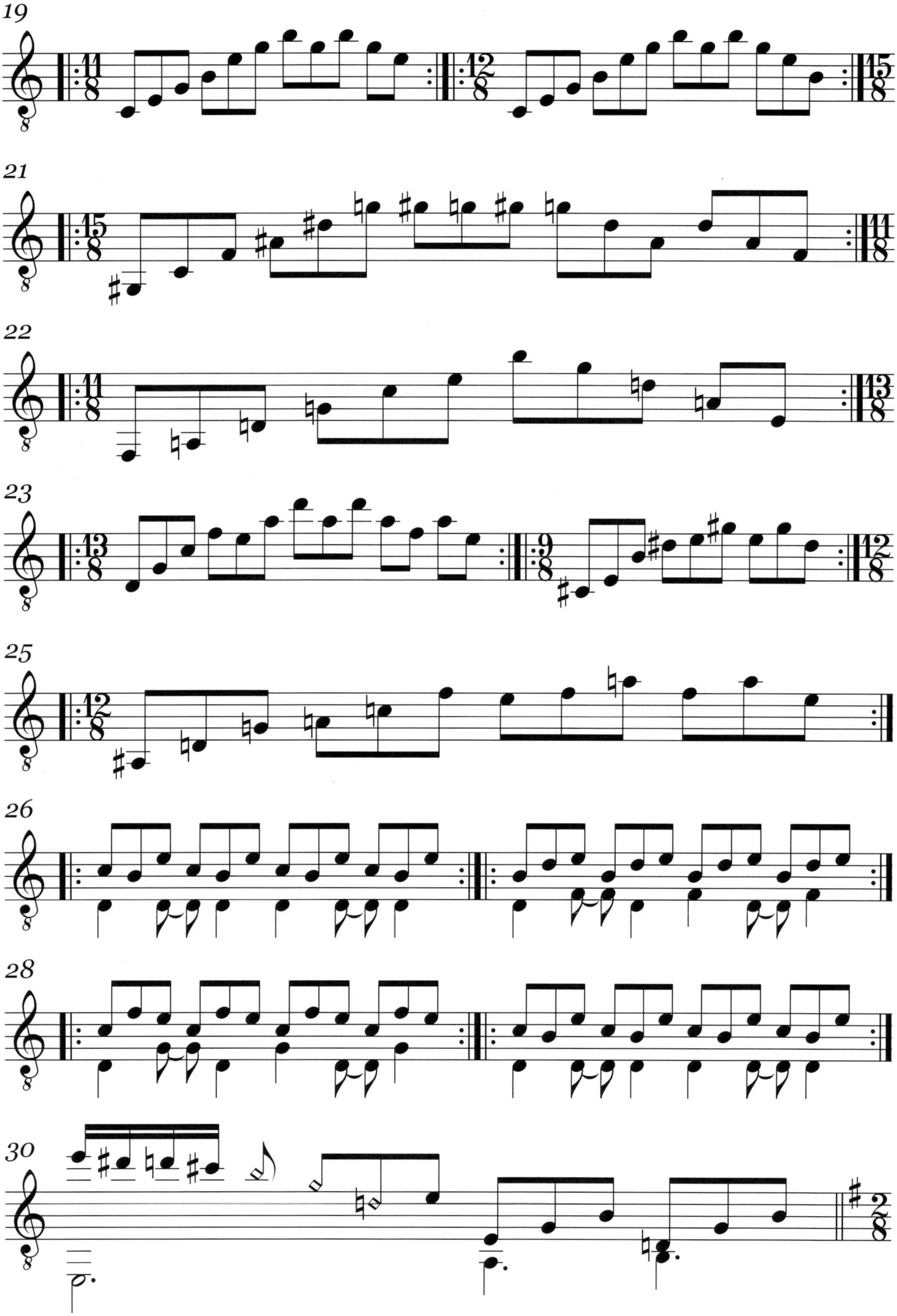
19
21
22
23
25
26
28
30

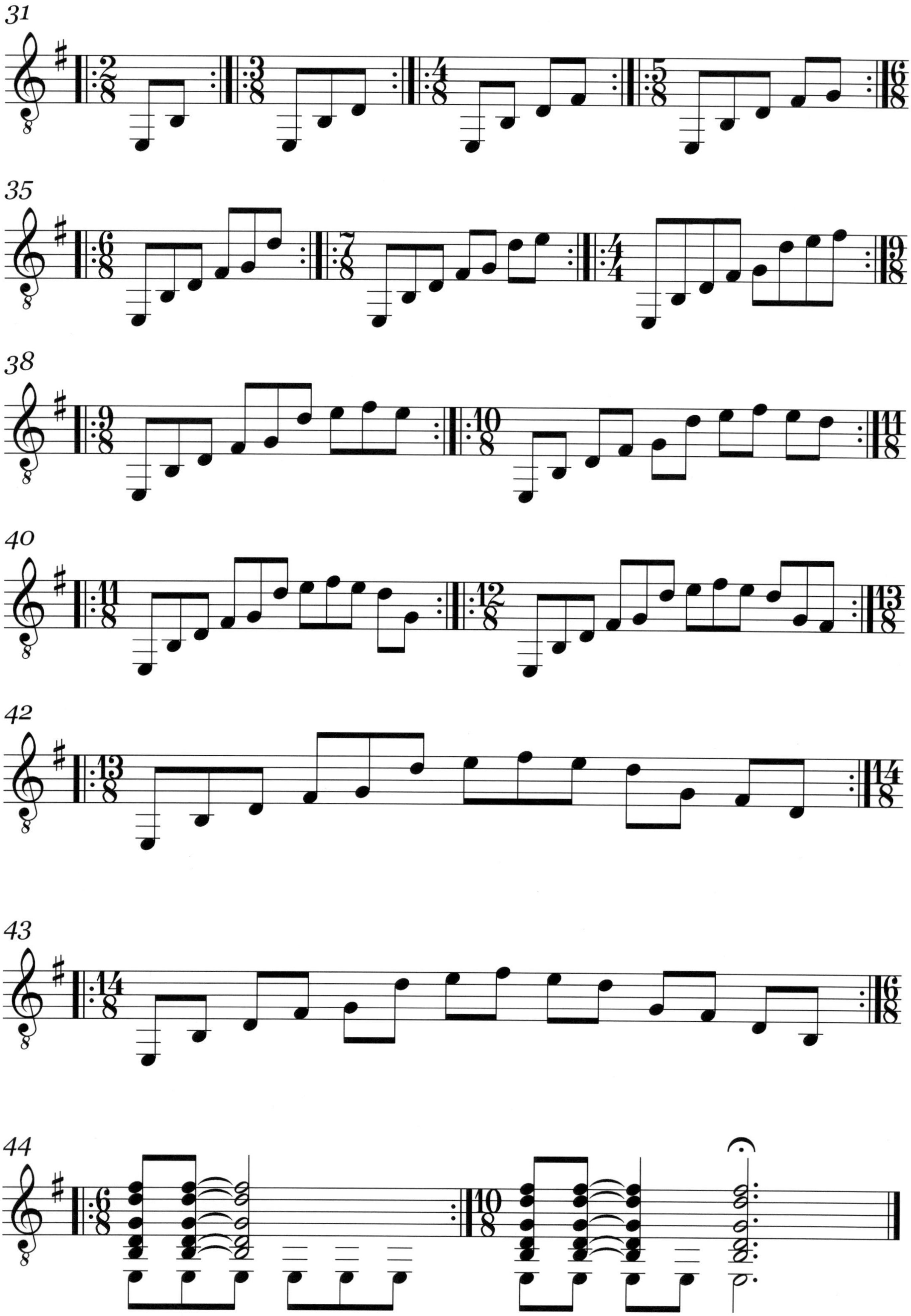

THREE GYMN O'PADDIES (2000-2001)

1. *To Erik Satie*

2. *For Erik Satie*

3. *Á Erik Satie*

Three Gymn O'Paddies

To Erik Satie

Gymn O'Paddy No.1

The dynamics shown are just guidelines.
Use your imagination in your interpretation.
Generally let melody notes ring across strings.

Dave Flynn
Dublin, Dec 2000

Slowly, with Irish wisdom

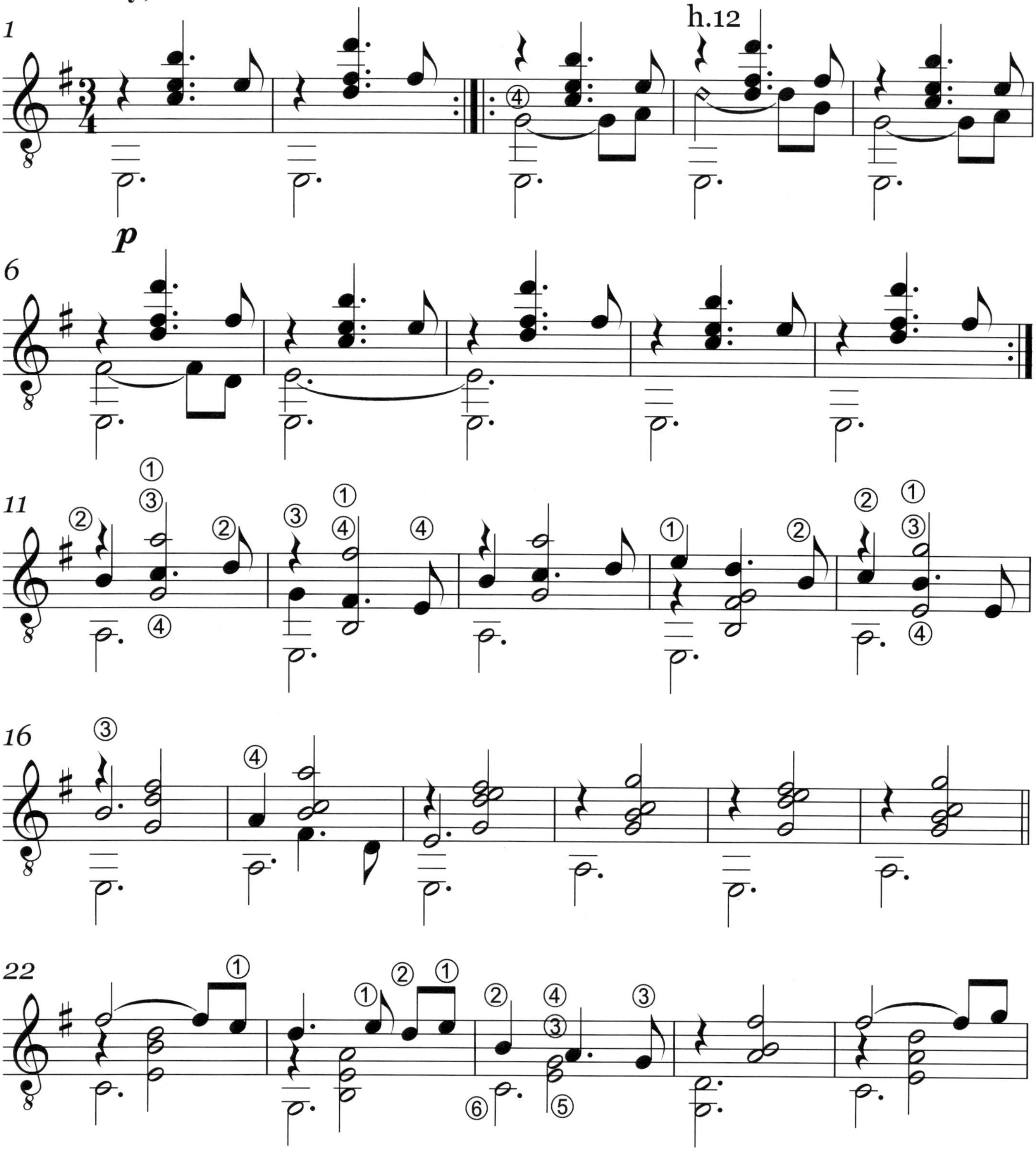

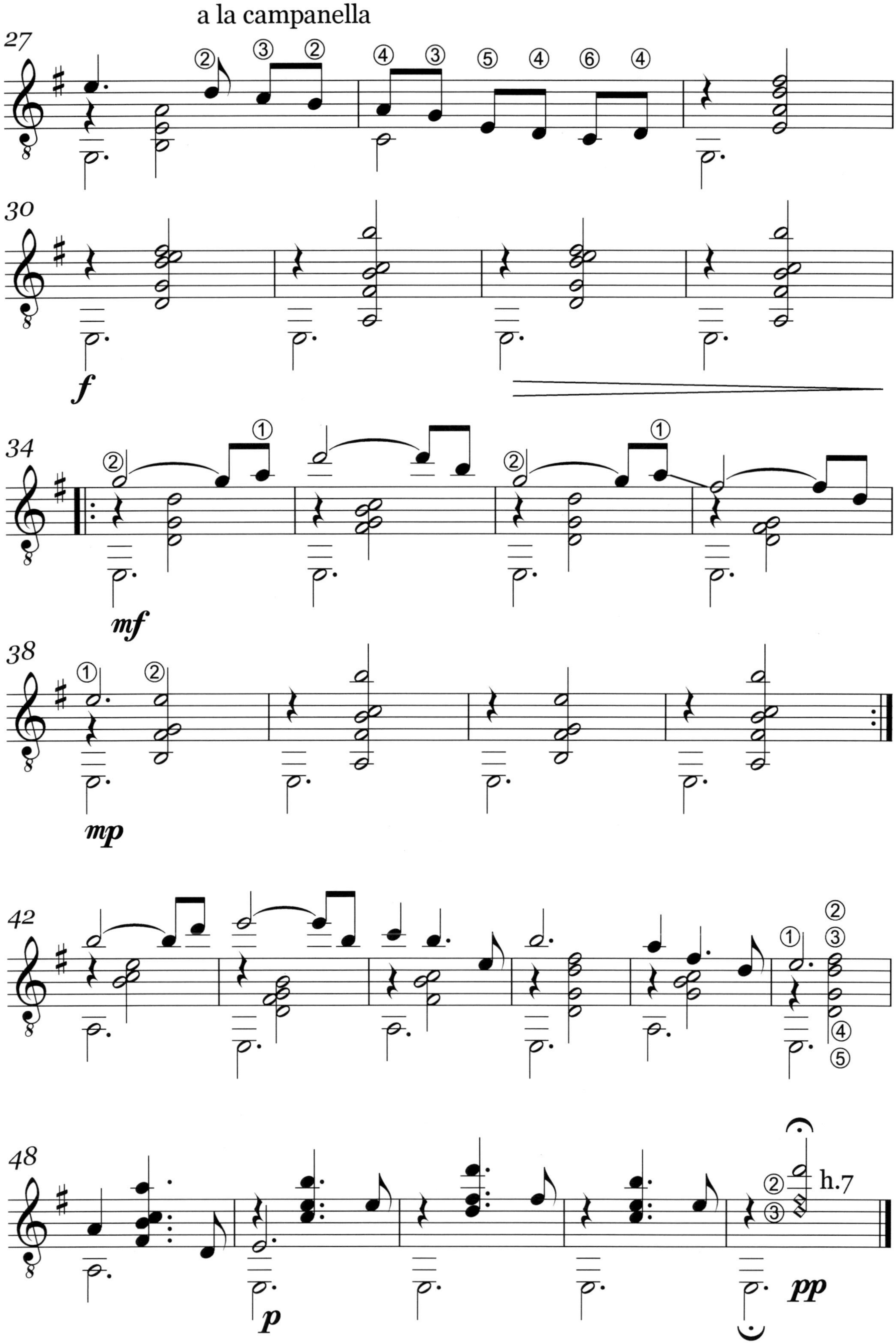
a la campanella
27
30
f
34
mf
38
mp
42
48
p
h.7
pp

for Erik Satie

Gymn O'Paddy No.2

Slowly with Celtic mysticism

Dave Flynn
Dublin 2000

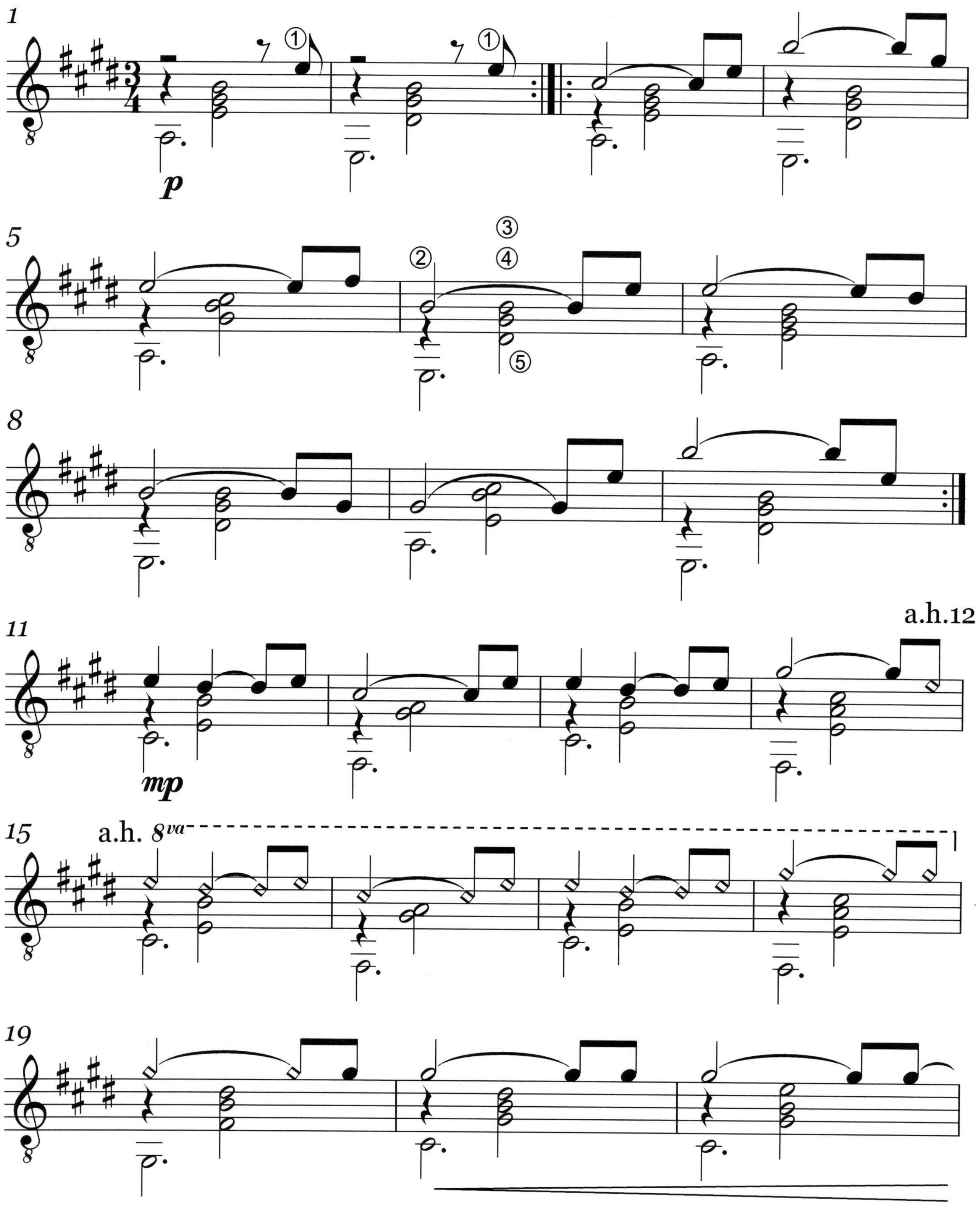

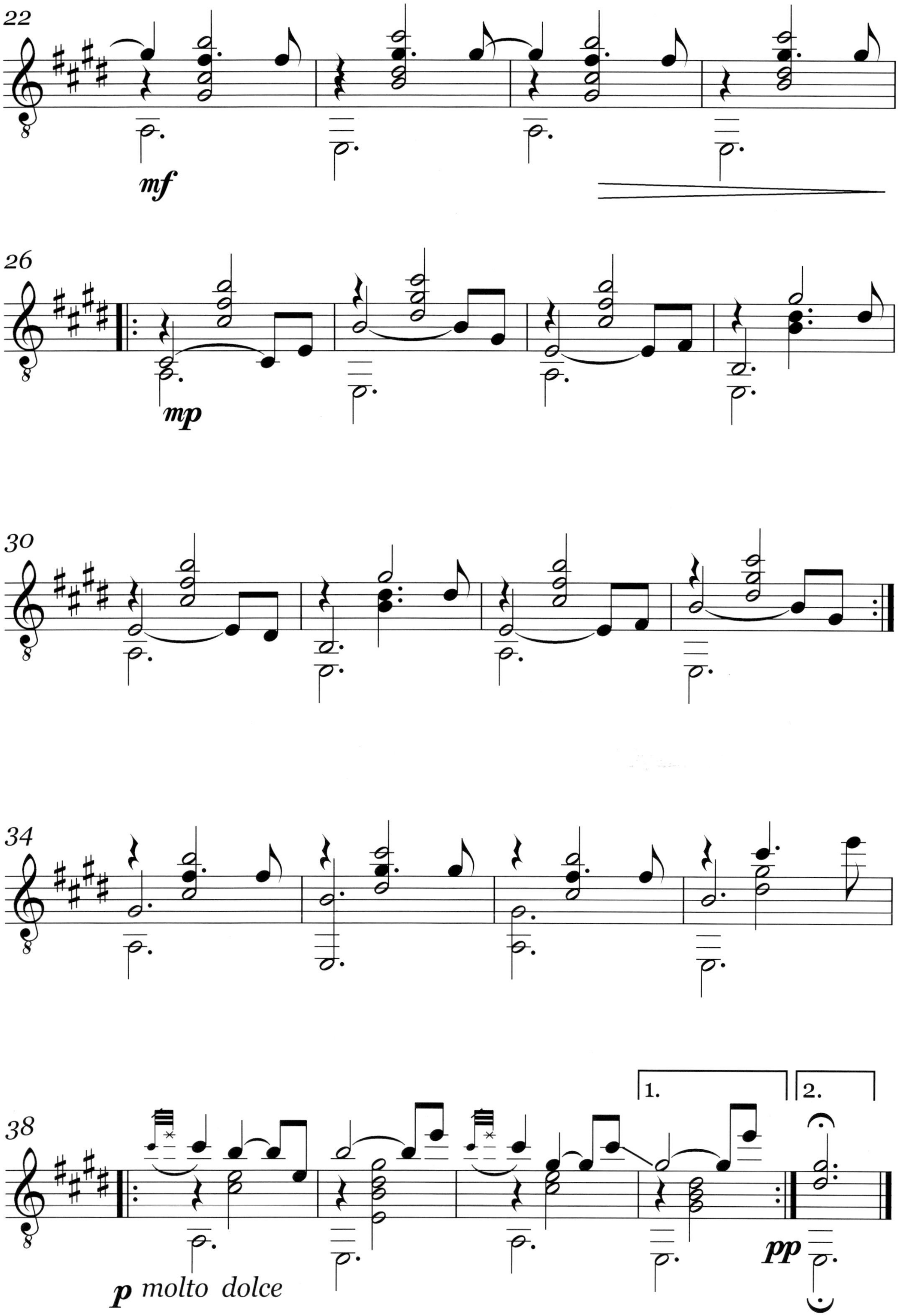

22
mf
26
mp
30
34
38
p molto dolce
1.
2.
pp

á Erik Satie

Gymn O'Paddy No.3

Slowly, with Gaelic charm

Dave Flynn
Dublin, June 2001

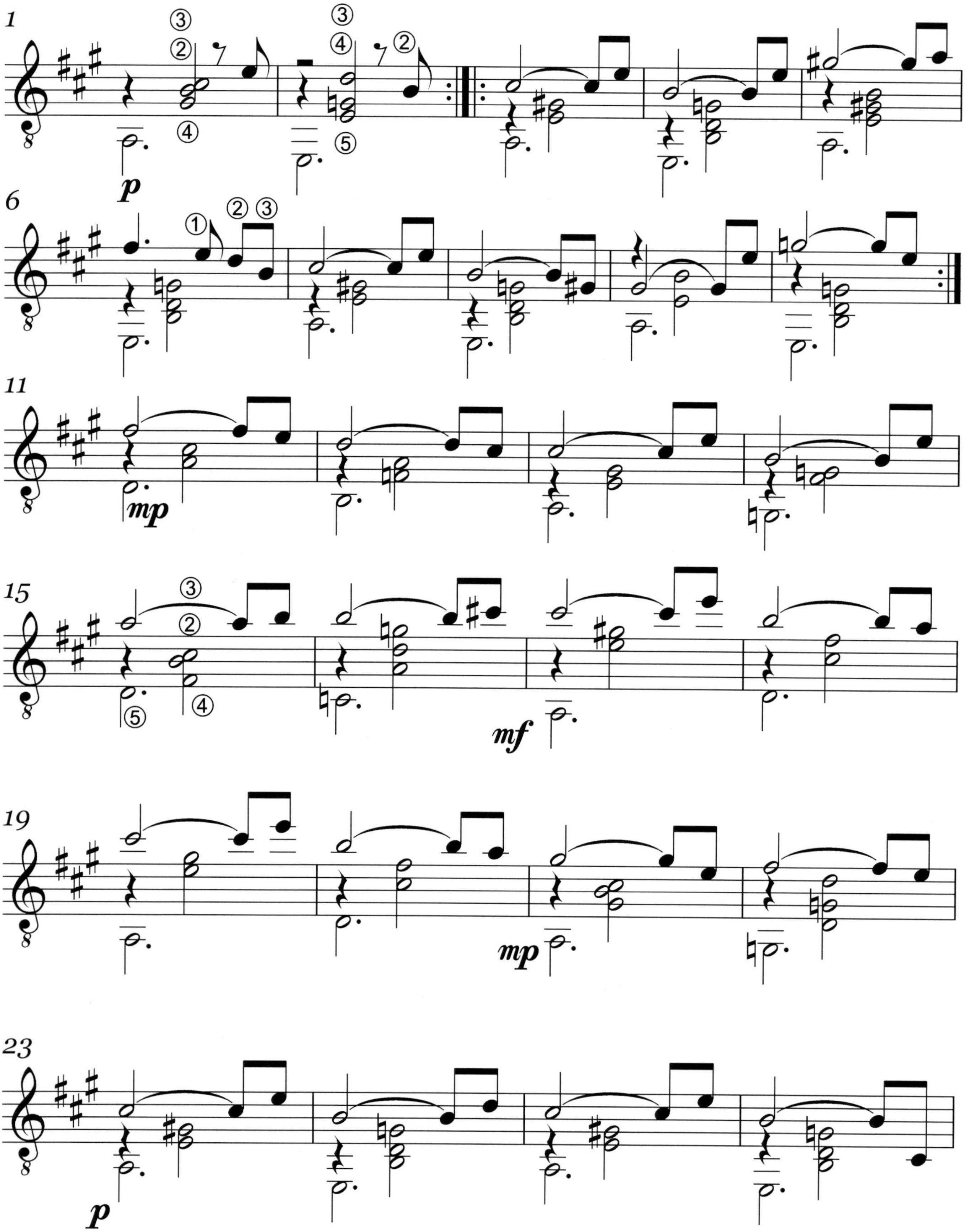

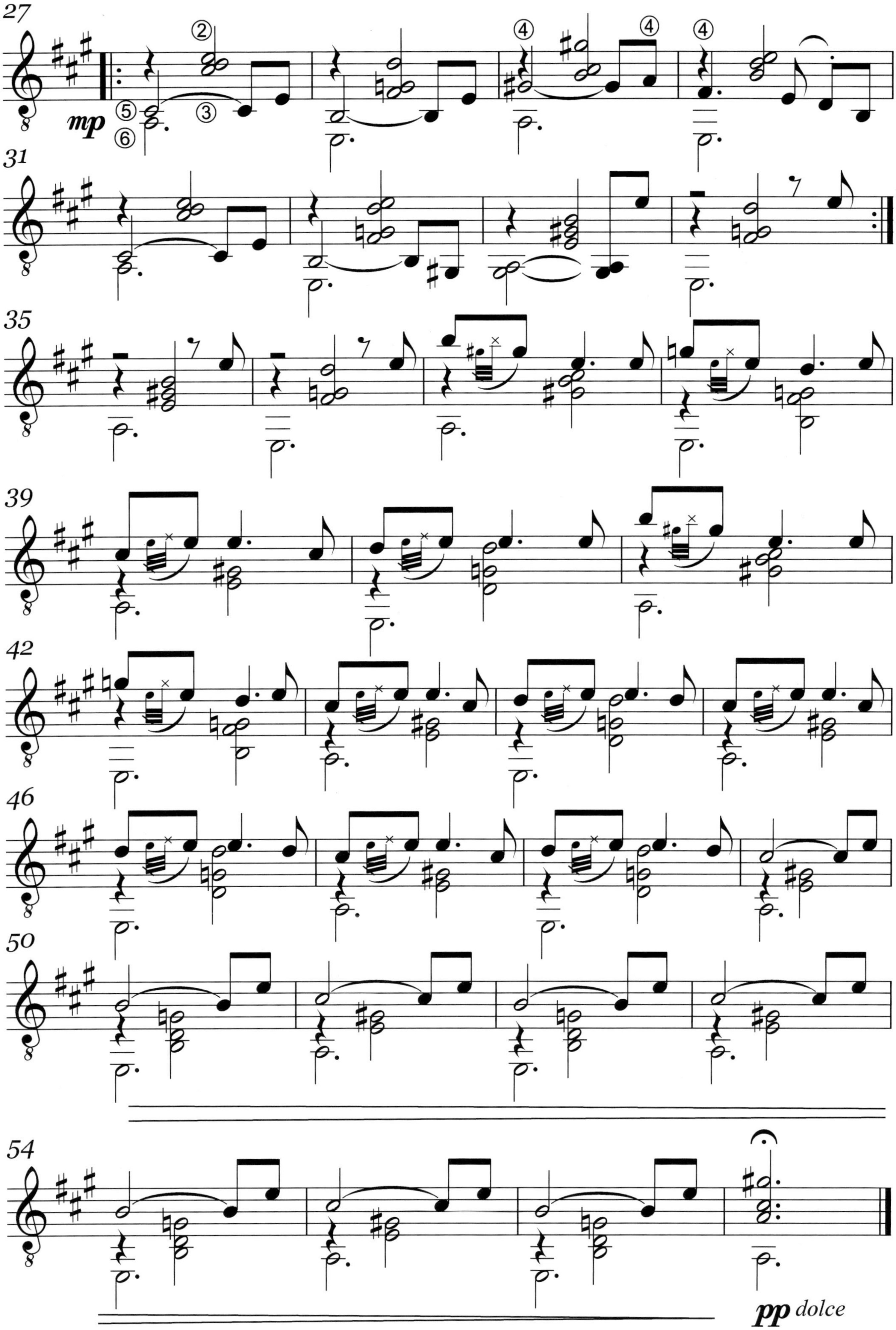
27
mp
31
35
39
42
46
50
54
pp dolce

HOMAGE SONATINA (1993-2001)

I
Homage to Villa-Lobos

II
Elegy for Joan
(Homage to Andy Summers)

III
Irish Seascape with Waves
(Homage to Leo Brouwer)

Homage Sonatina
I. Homage to Villa-Lobos

Dave Flynn
Dublin, 1998

Use open strings where possible throughout
and let notes ring into each other.

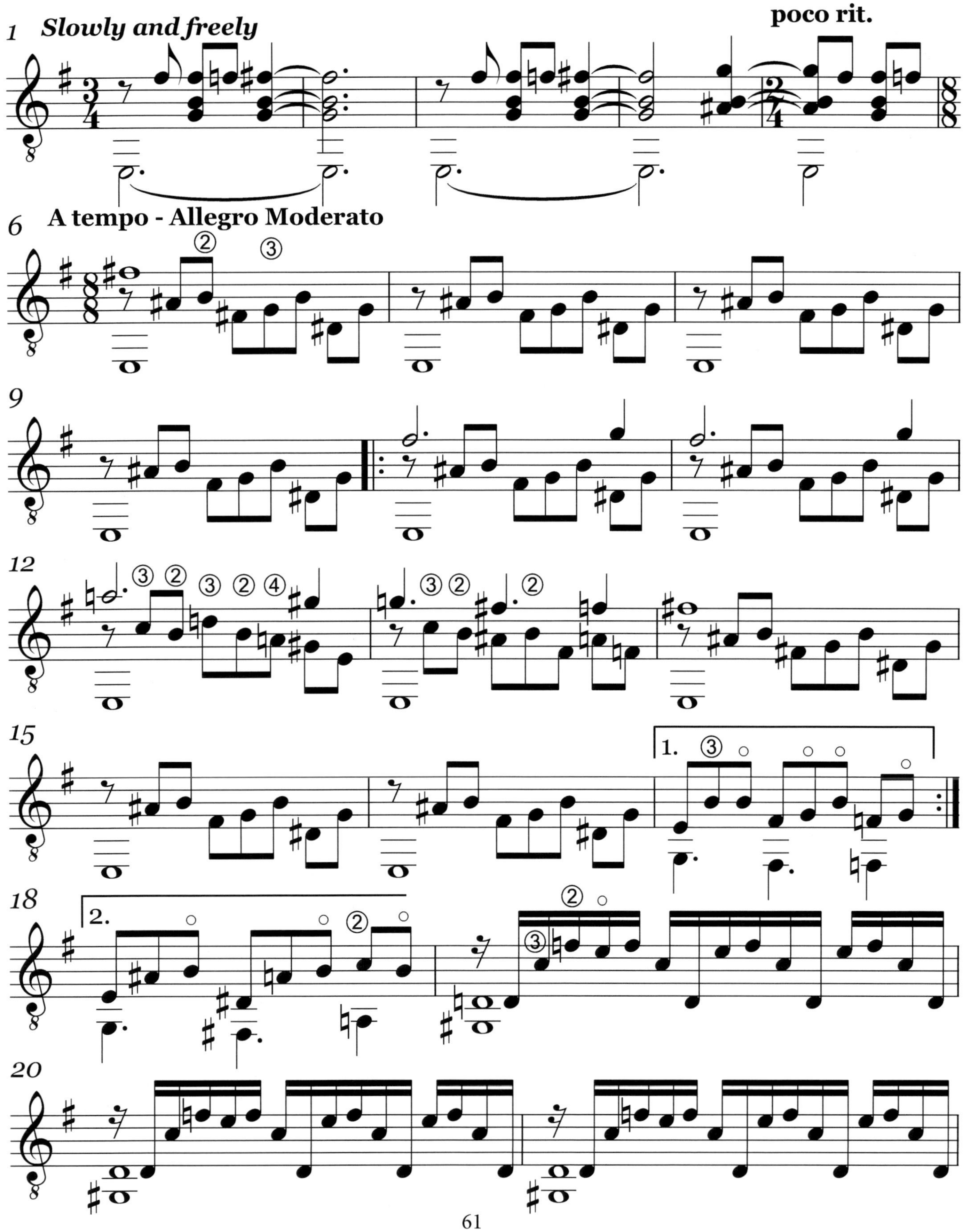

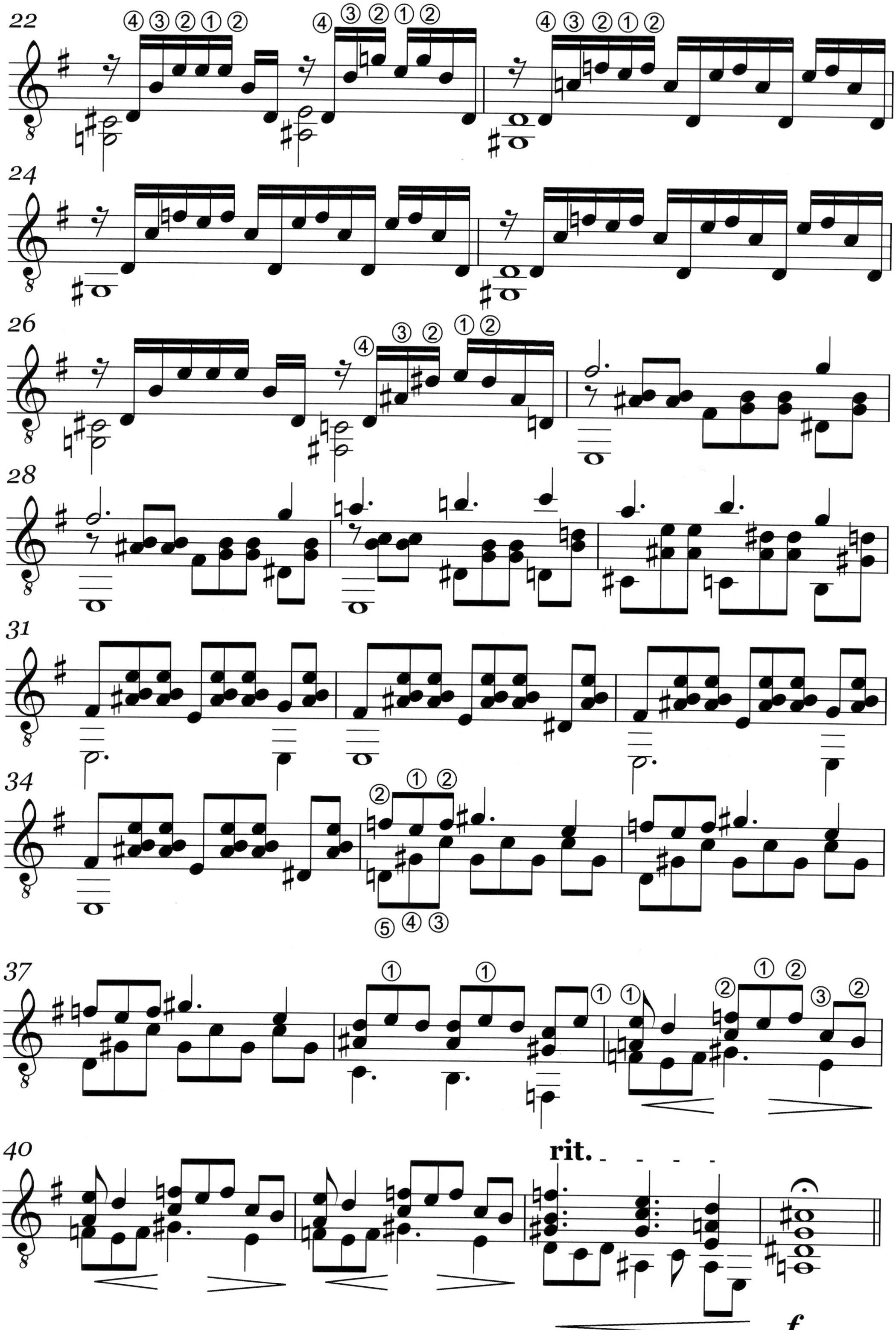
22
24
26
28
31
34
37
40
rit.
f

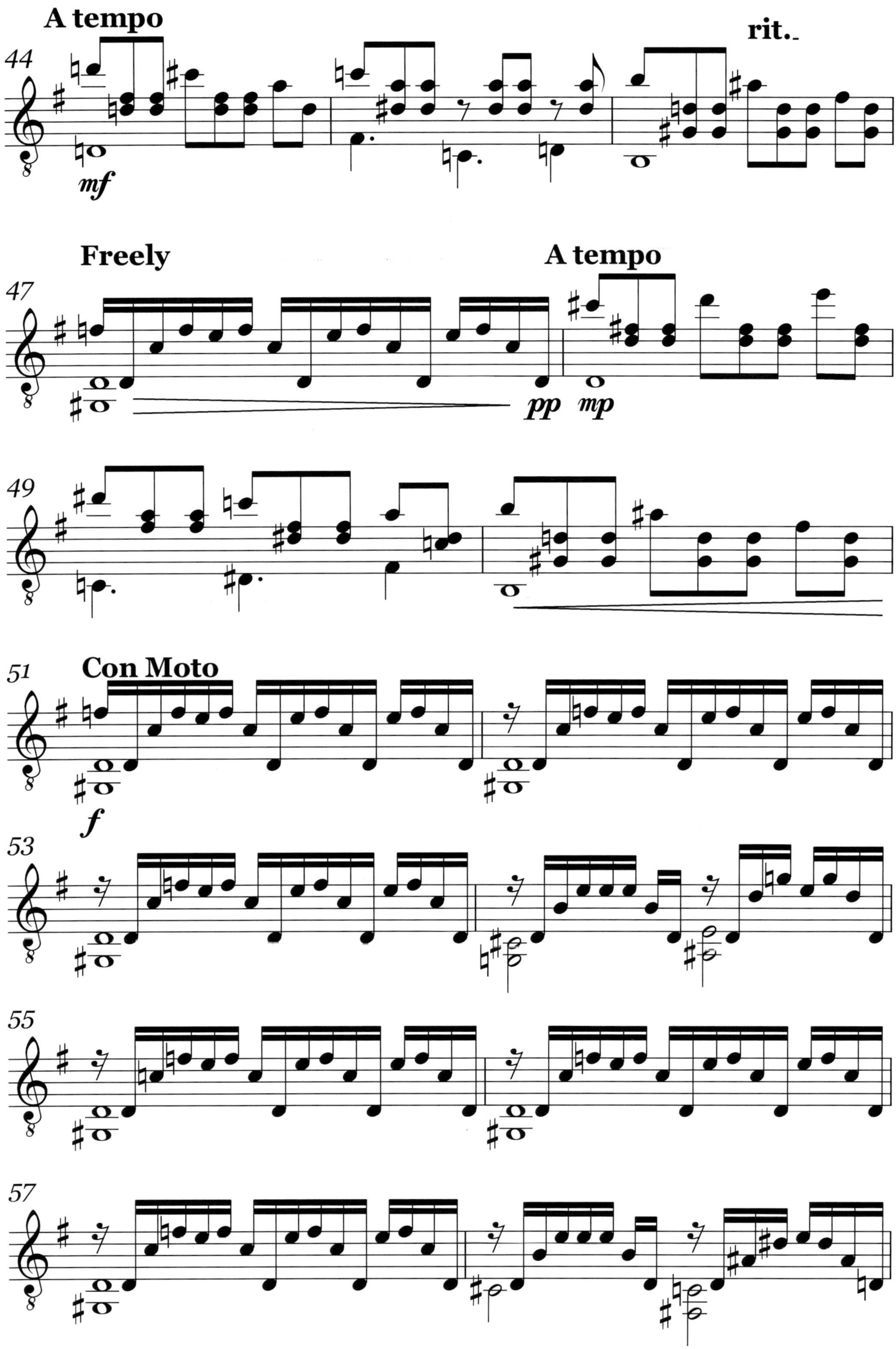
A tempo
44
mf
rit.
Freely
47
pp
A tempo
mp
49
51
Con Moto
f
53
55
57

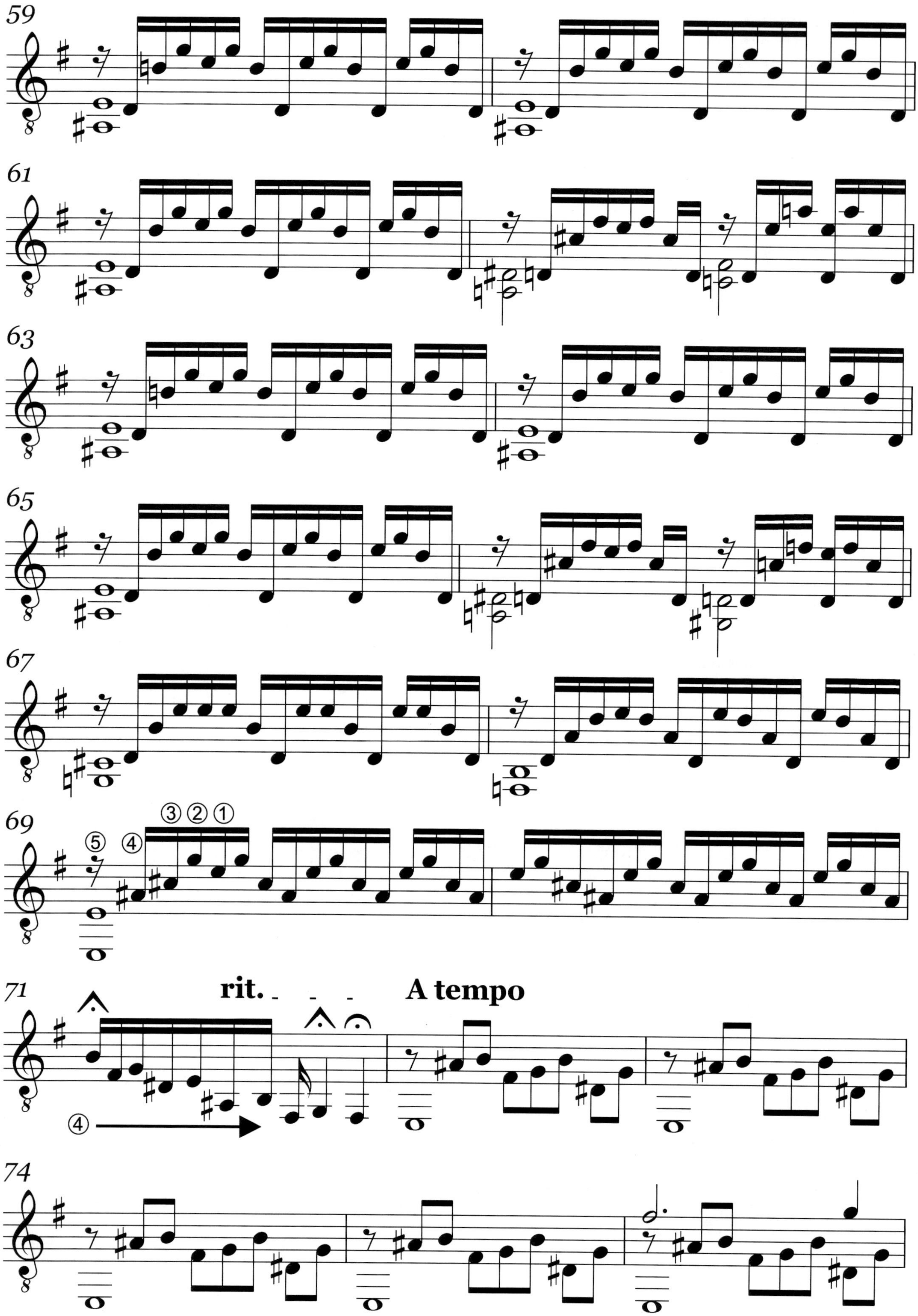
59
61
63
65
67
69
71
rit.
A tempo
74

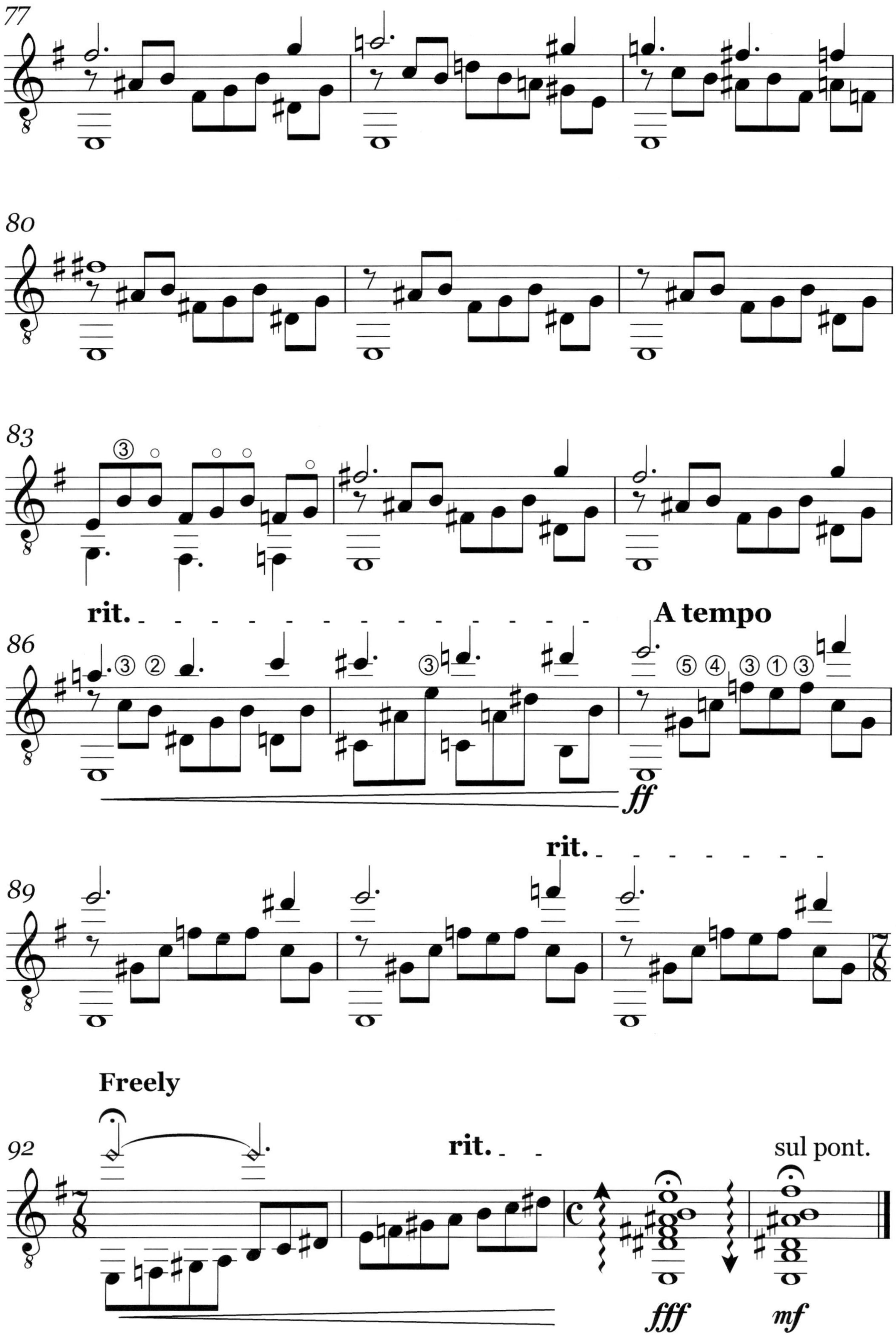
77
80
83
rit.
A tempo
86
ff
rit.
89
Freely
92
rit.
sul pont.
fff
mf

II. Elegy for Joan

(Homage to Andy Summers)

Dave Flynn
Dublin, 1993

Andante
In this piece phrase marks are indicated above notes
Do not mistake these for slurs or ties

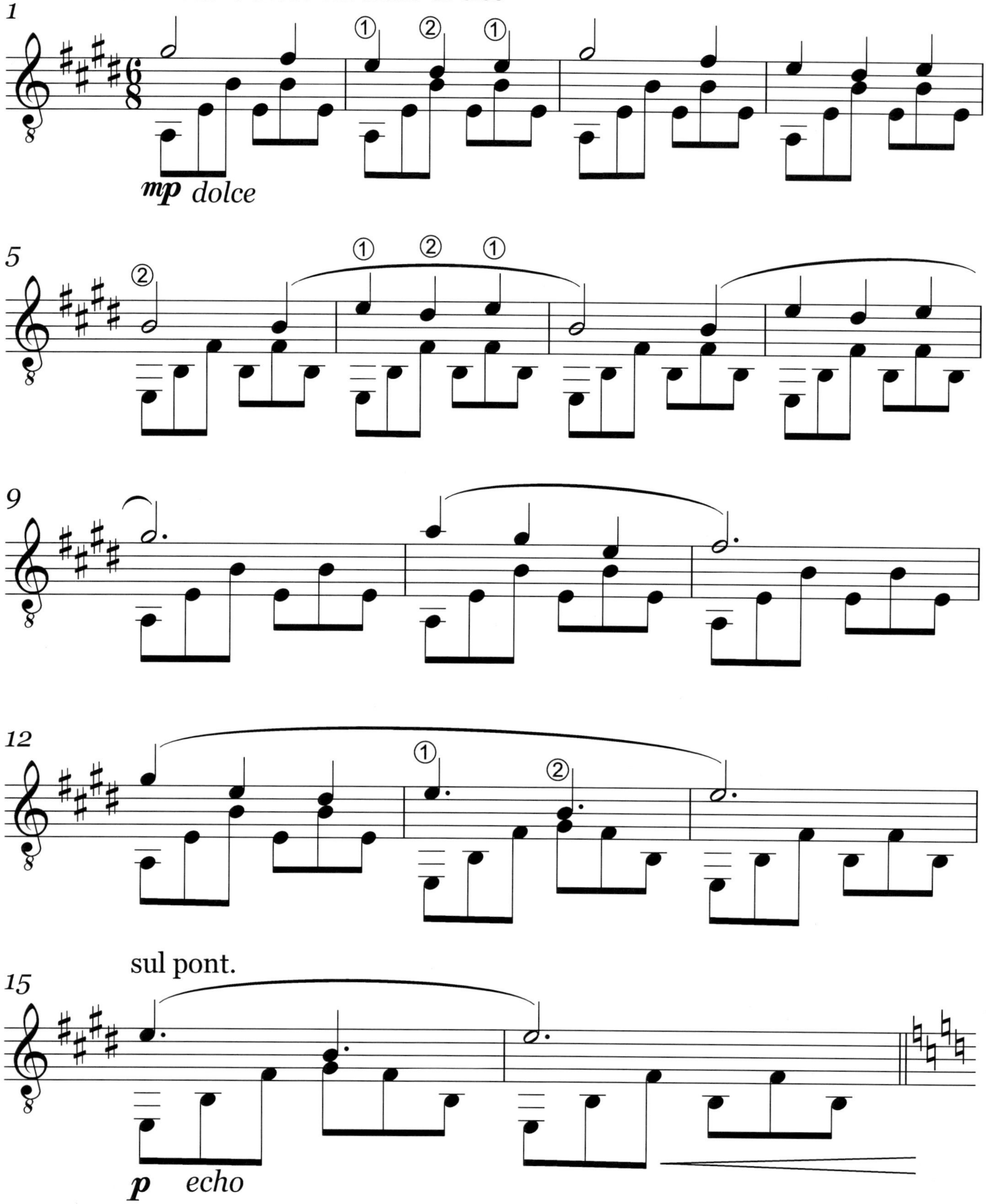

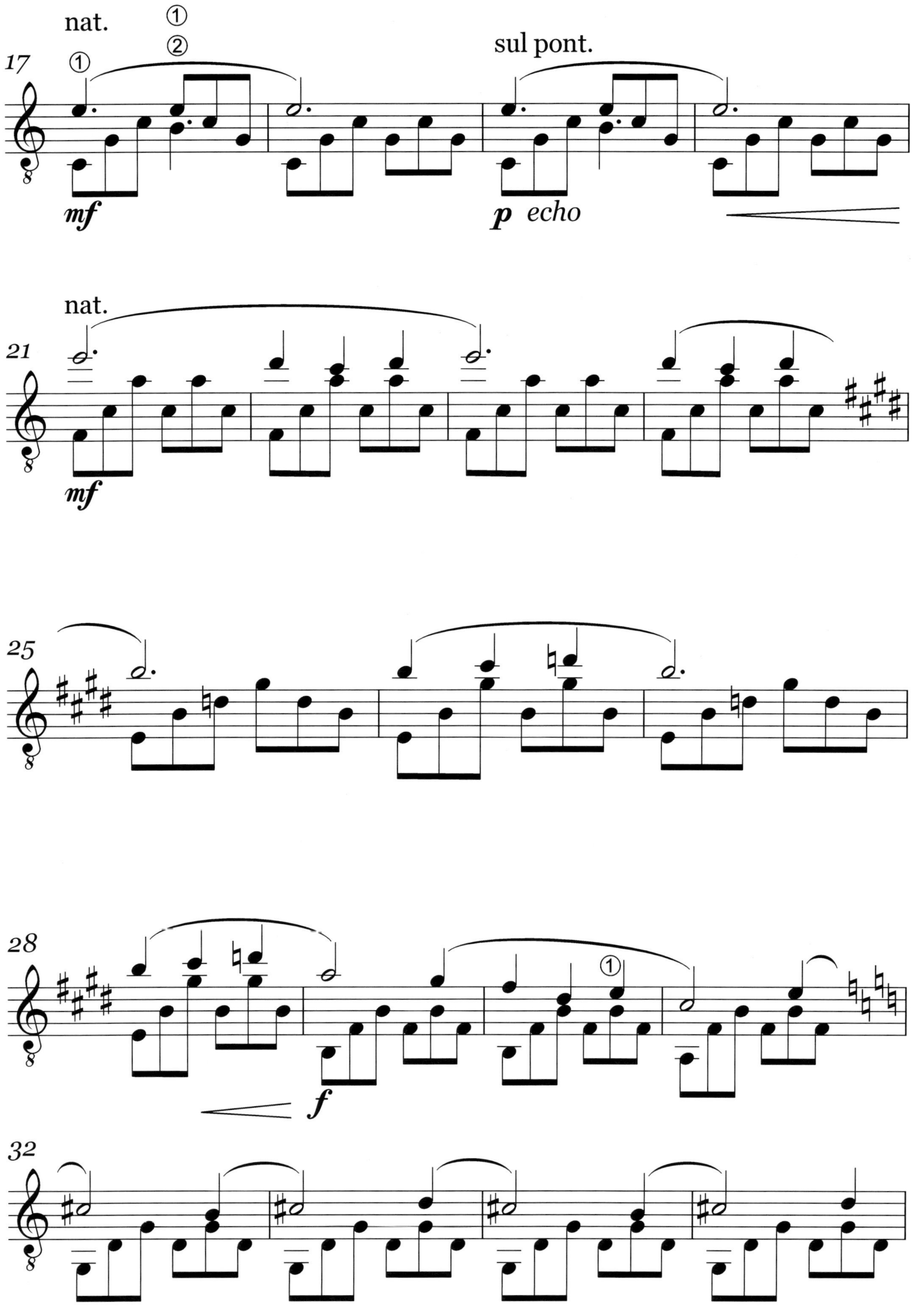
17
nat.
①
②
sul pont.
mf
p echo
21
nat.
mf
25
28
①
f
32

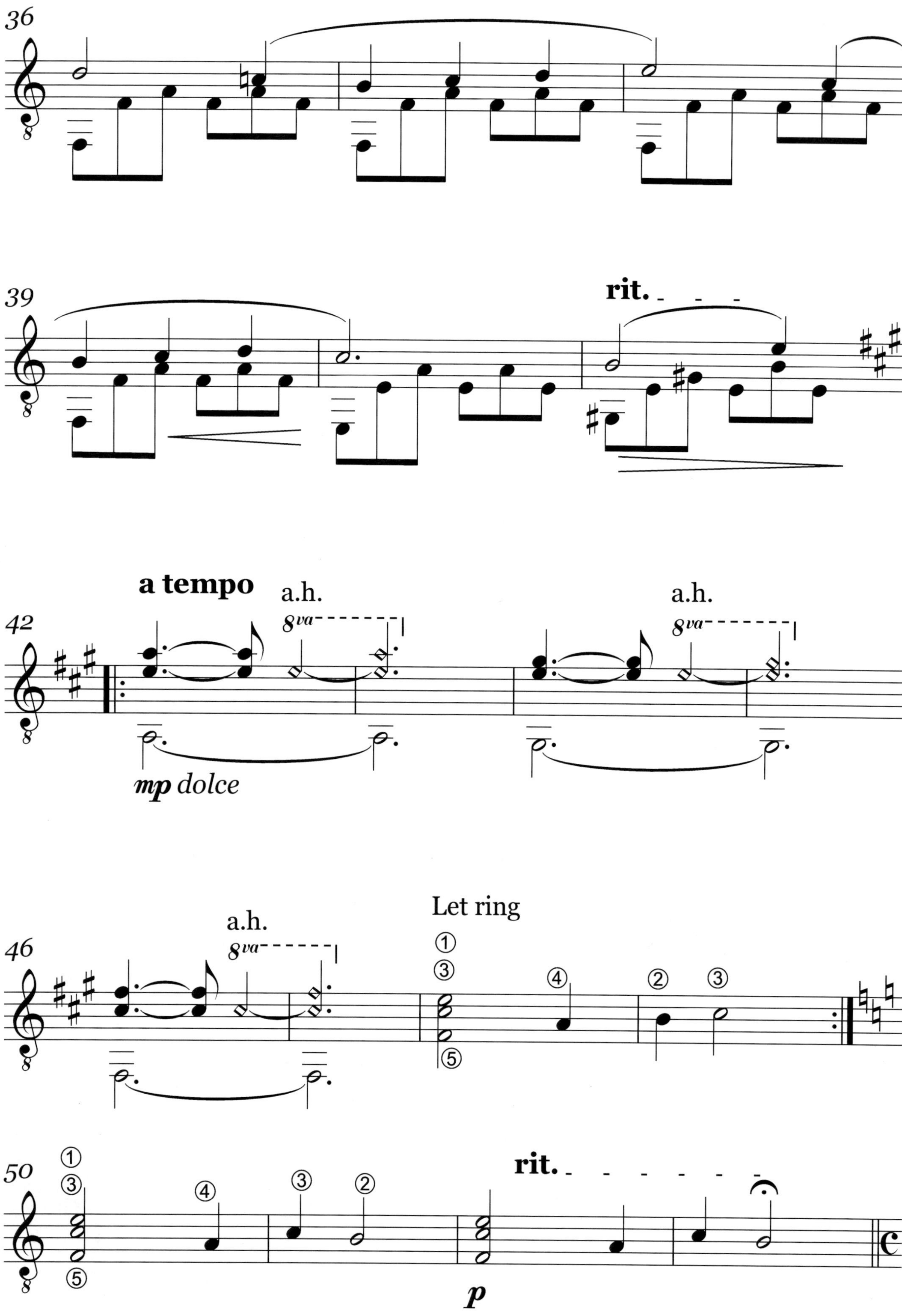
36
39
rit.
42
a tempo
a.h.
8va
mp dolce
a.h.
8va
46
a.h.
8va
Let ring
①
③
⑤
④
②
③
50
①
③
⑤
④
③
②
rit.
p

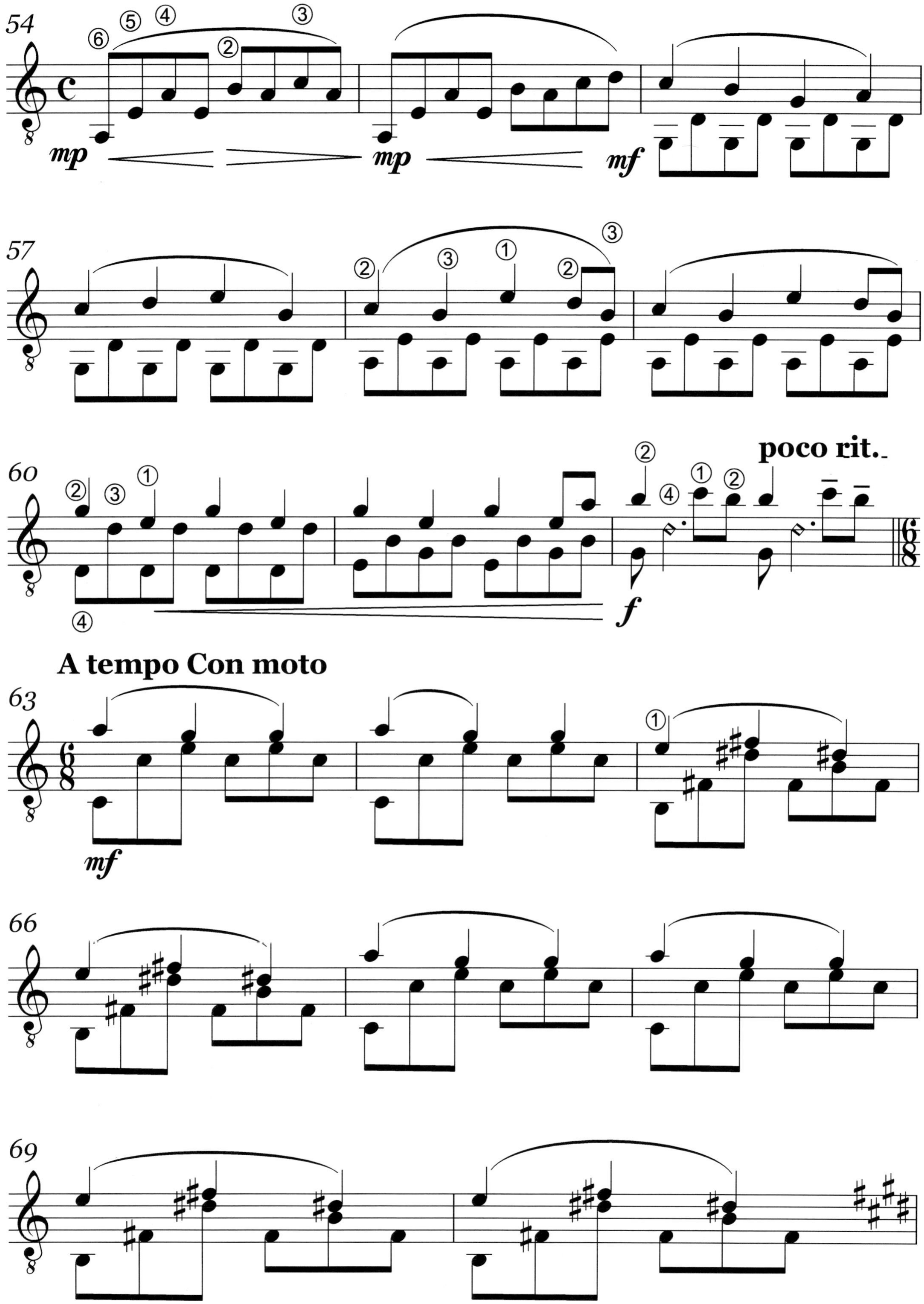
54
mp
mp
mf
57
60
f
poco rit.
A tempo Con moto
63
mf
66
69

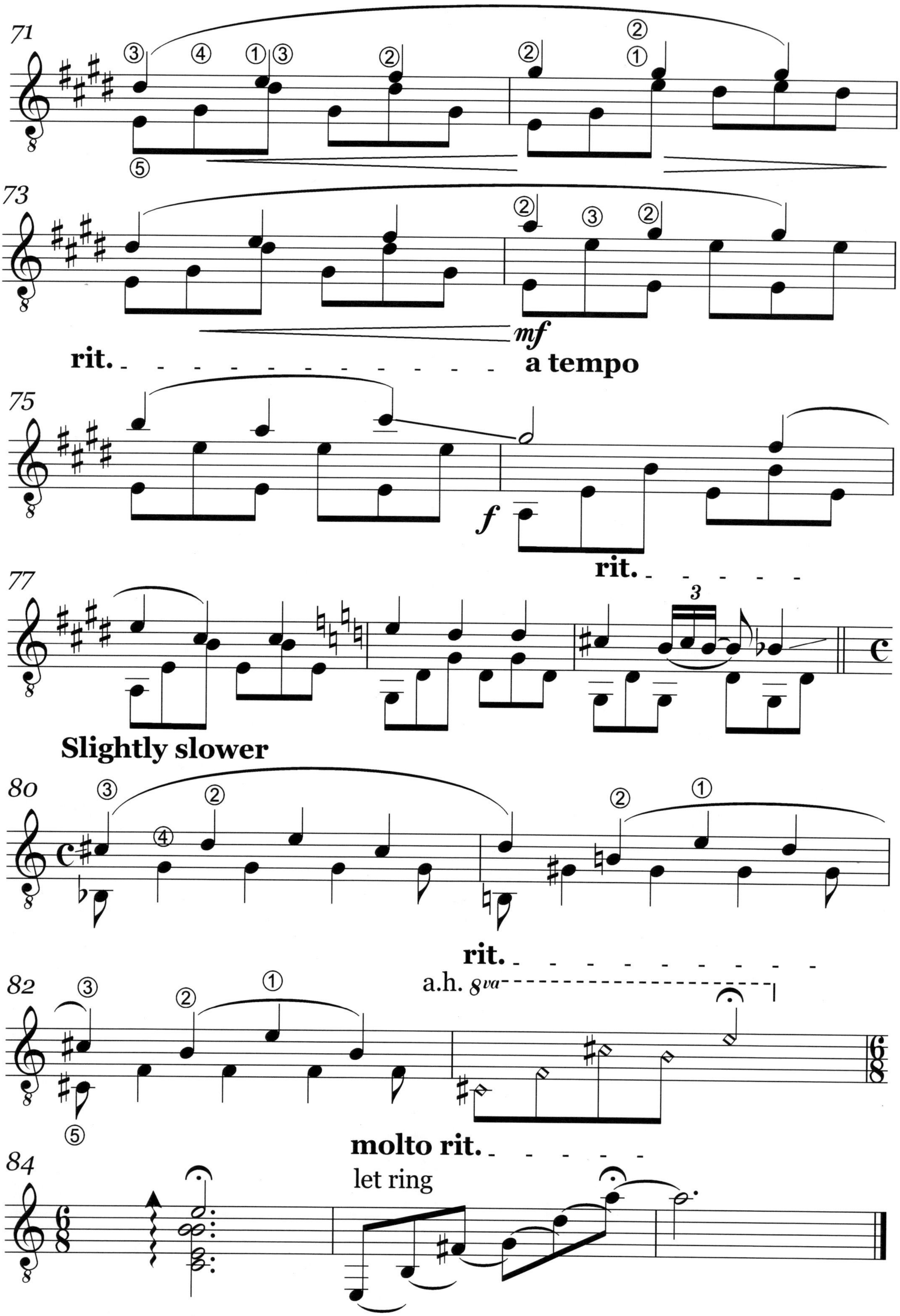
rit.
a tempo
rit.
Slightly slower
rit.
a.h. 8va
molto rit.
let ring

III. Irish Seascape With Waves

(Homage to Leo Brouwer)

Dave Flynn
Dublin, January 2001

NOTATION GUIDE

strum strings behind the nut — **muffle strings against fretboard at tenth fret** — **Hit open strings with right hand near the bridge Like a tamboura**

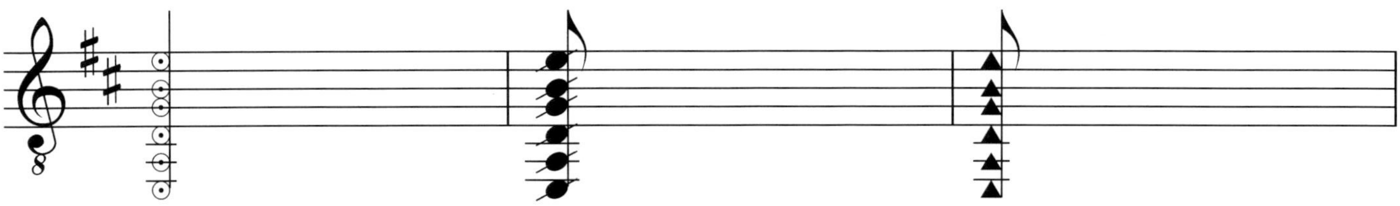

tap wood on side of guitar below the high E string — **tap notes with left hand finger** — **slap chord onto the fretboard with left hand first finger**

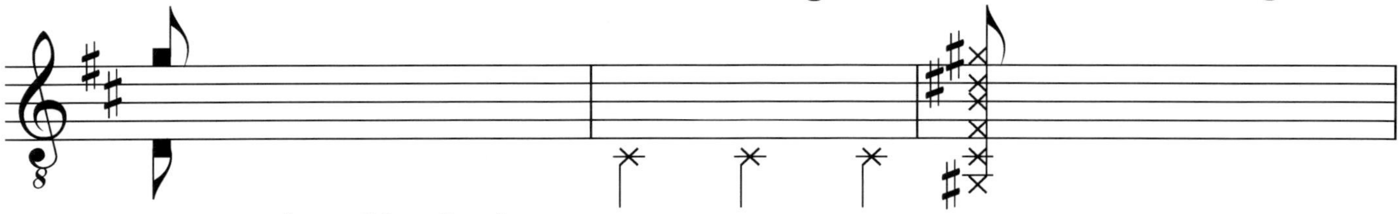

tap wood on side of guitar below the low E string

while holding onto the chord with left hand, strum directly behind the fretted chord with the right hand — **tap bass notes with left hand and treble notes with right hand**

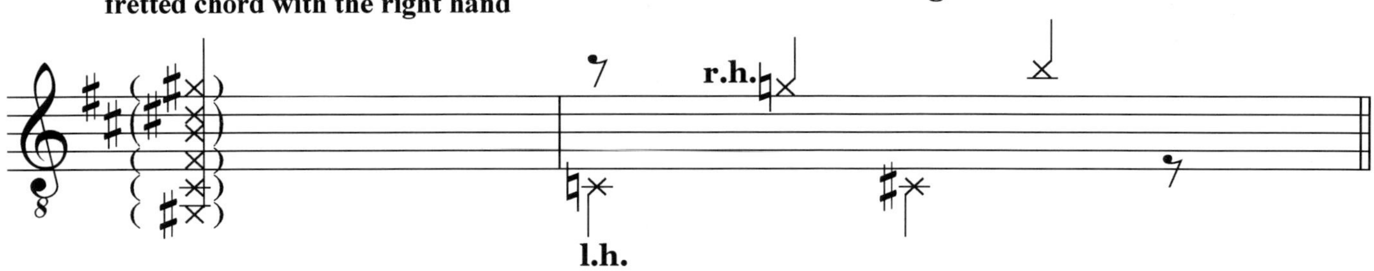

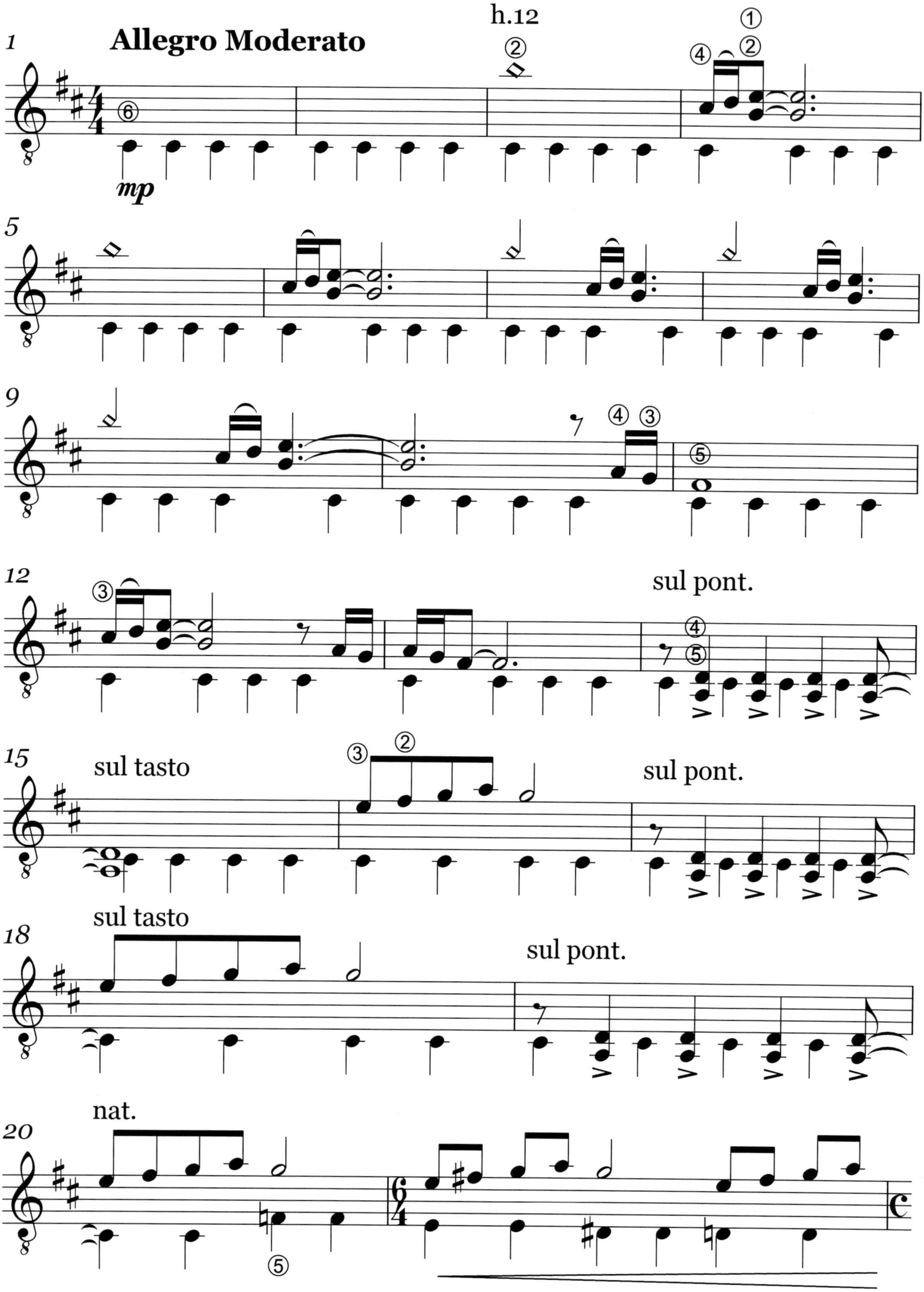
Allegro Moderato
h.12
mp
sul pont.
sul tasto
sul pont.
sul tasto
sul pont.
nat.

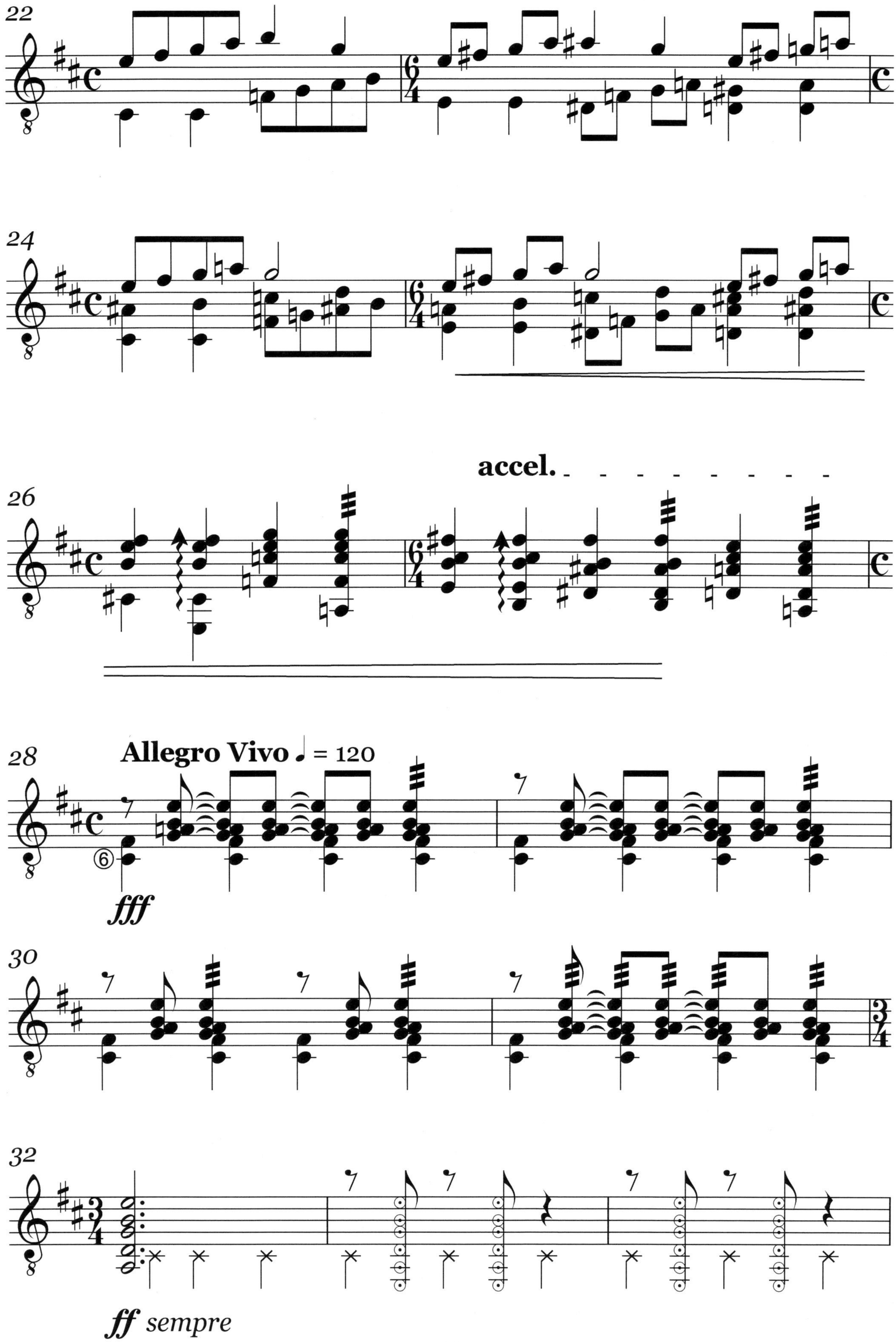
accel.
Allegro Vivo ♩ = 120
fff
ff sempre

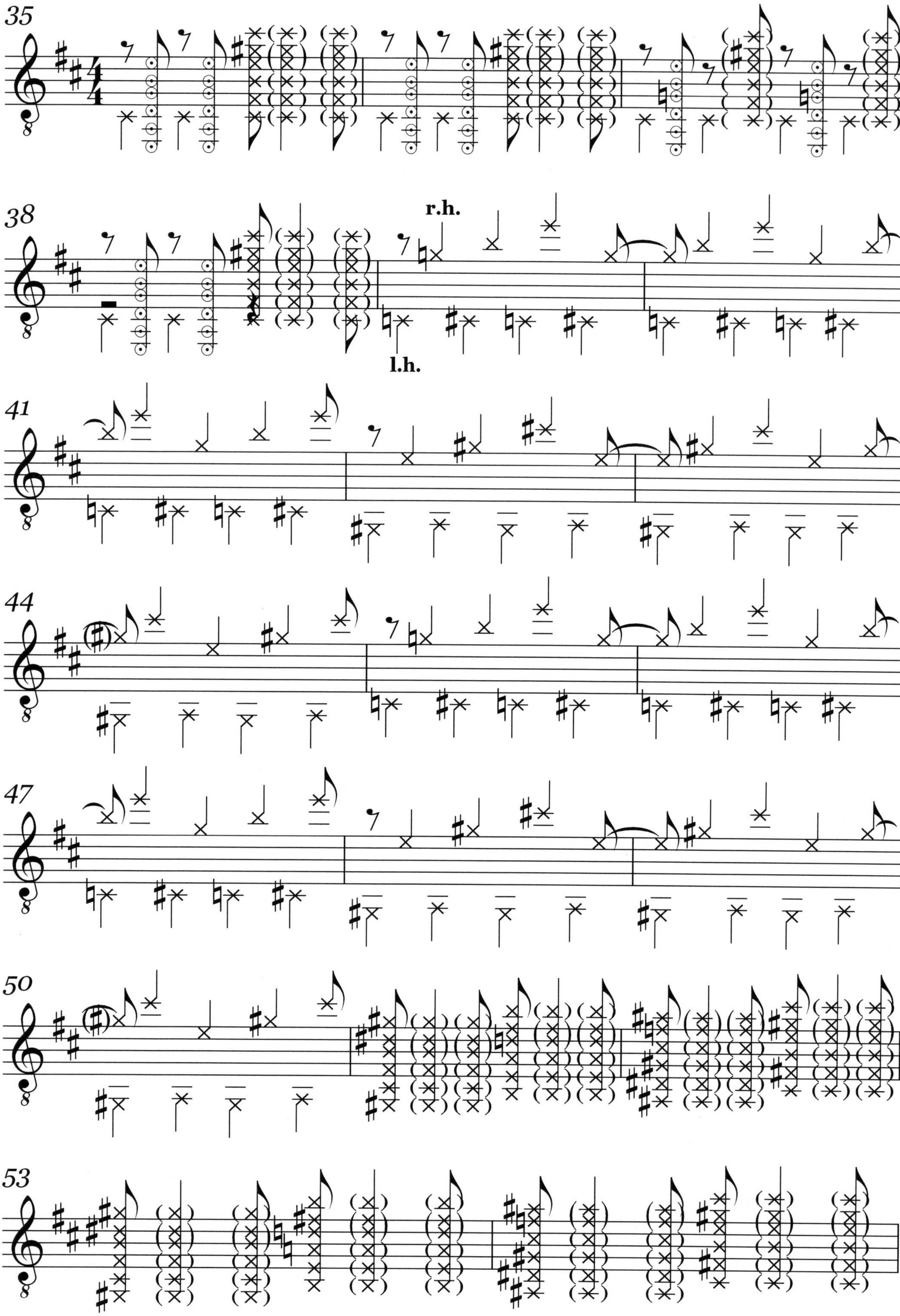
35
38
r.h.
l.h.
41
44
47
50
53

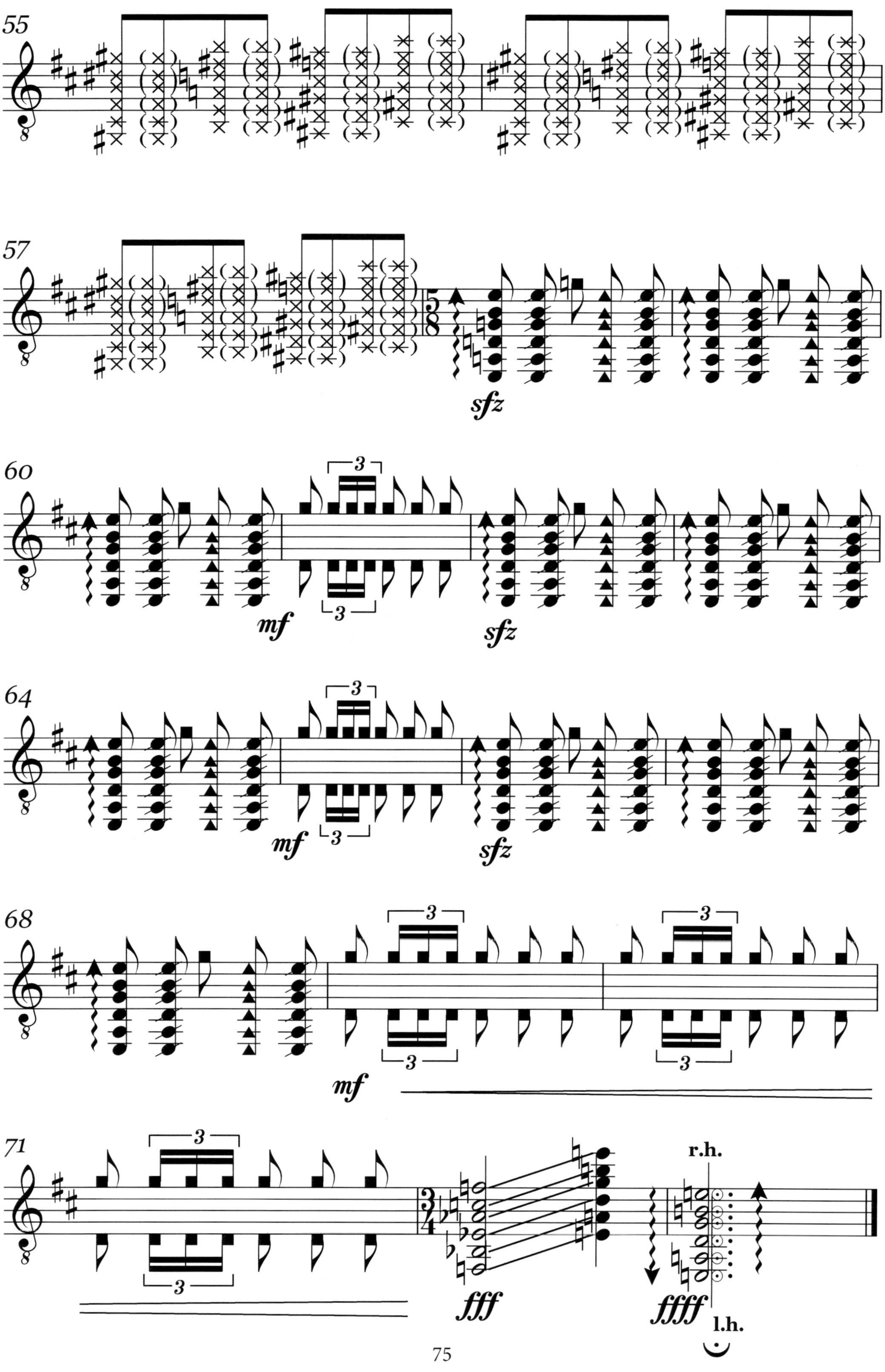
55
57
sfz
60
mf
sfz
64
mf
sfz
68
mf
71
fff
r.h.
ffff
l.h.

This page has been left blank to avoid an awkward page turn.

PASSACAGLIA (2000)

PASSACAGLIA

Dave Flynn
Dublin, 2000

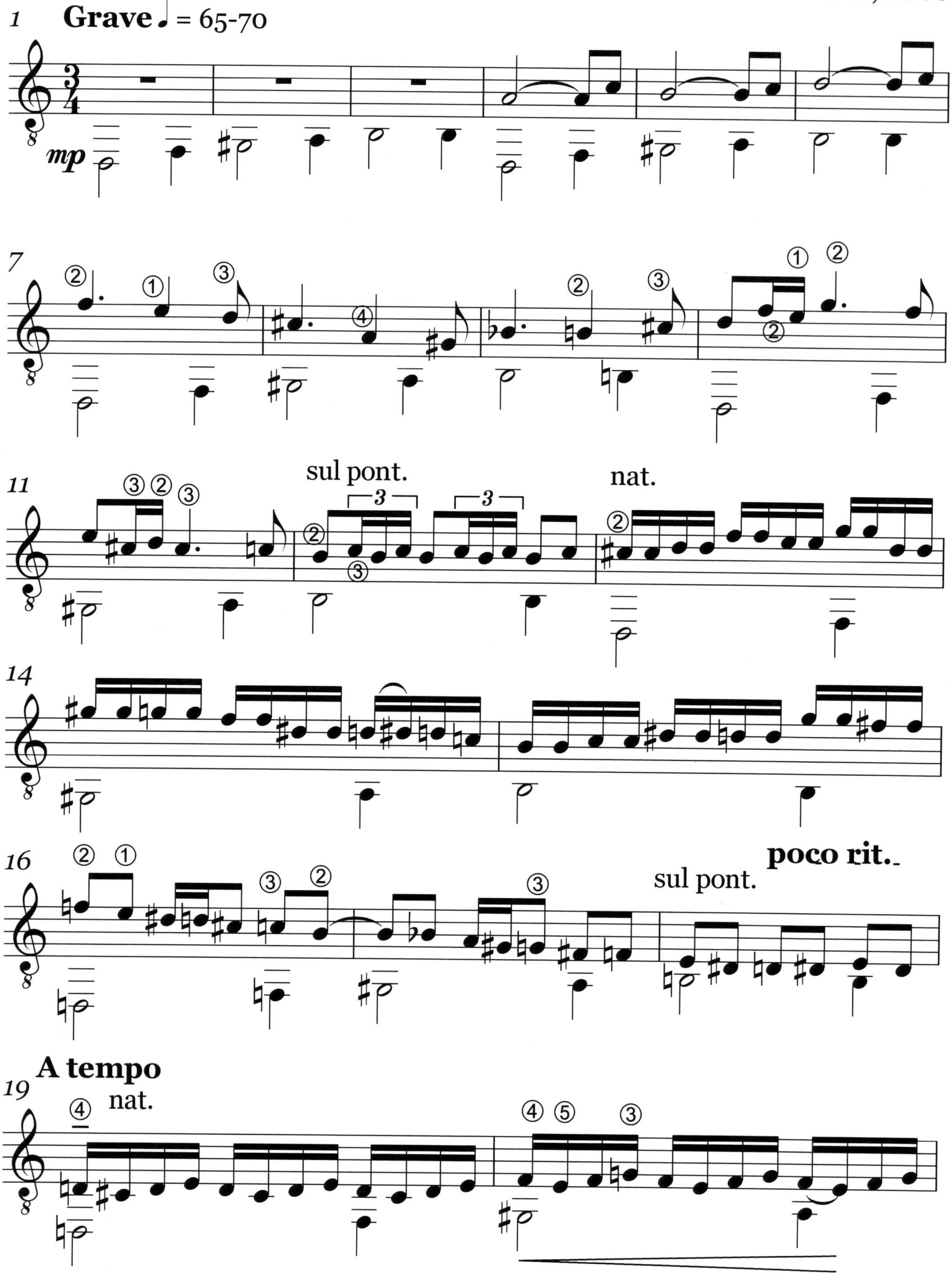

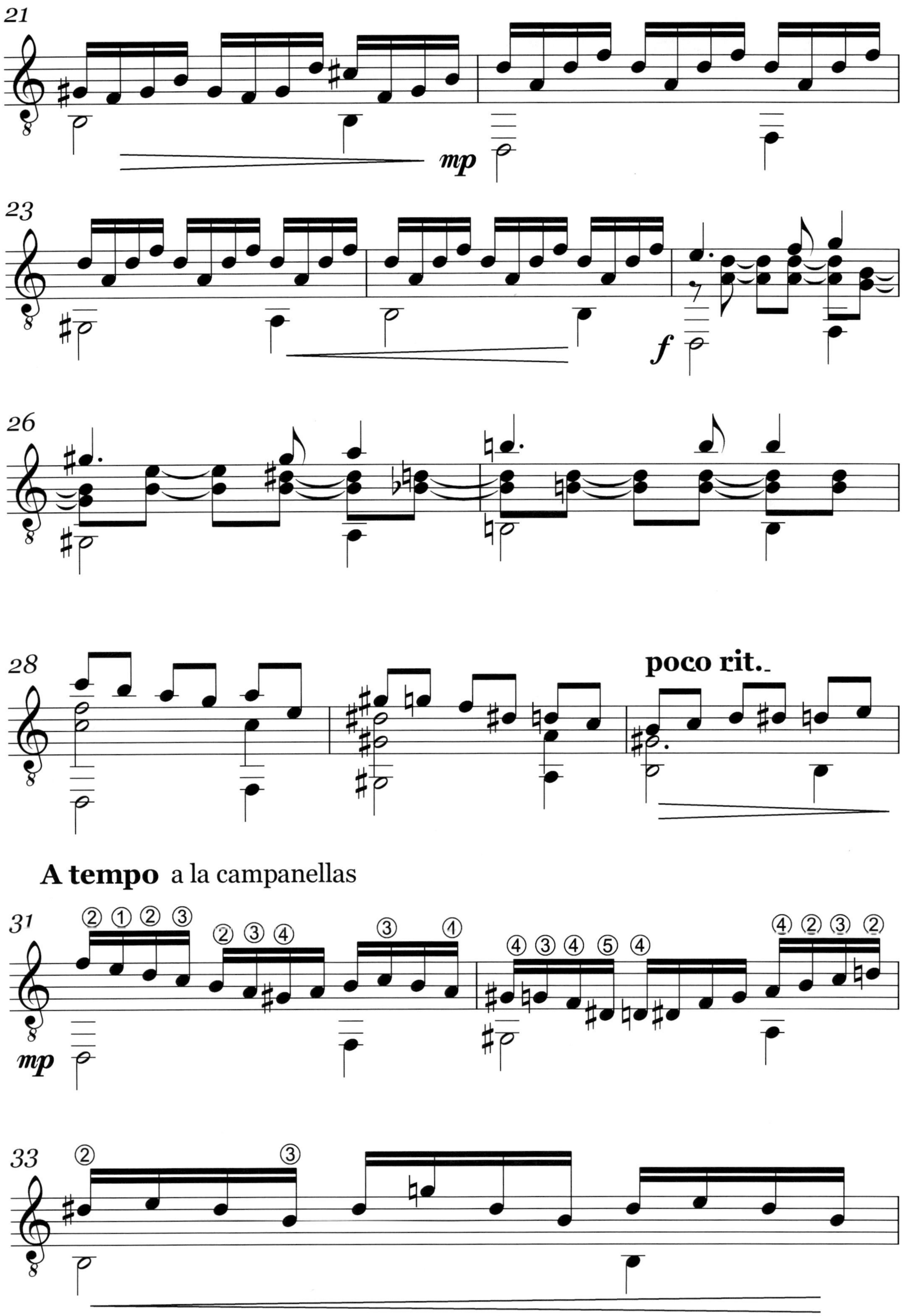
21
mp
23
f
26
28
poco rit.
A tempo a la campanellas
31
mp
33

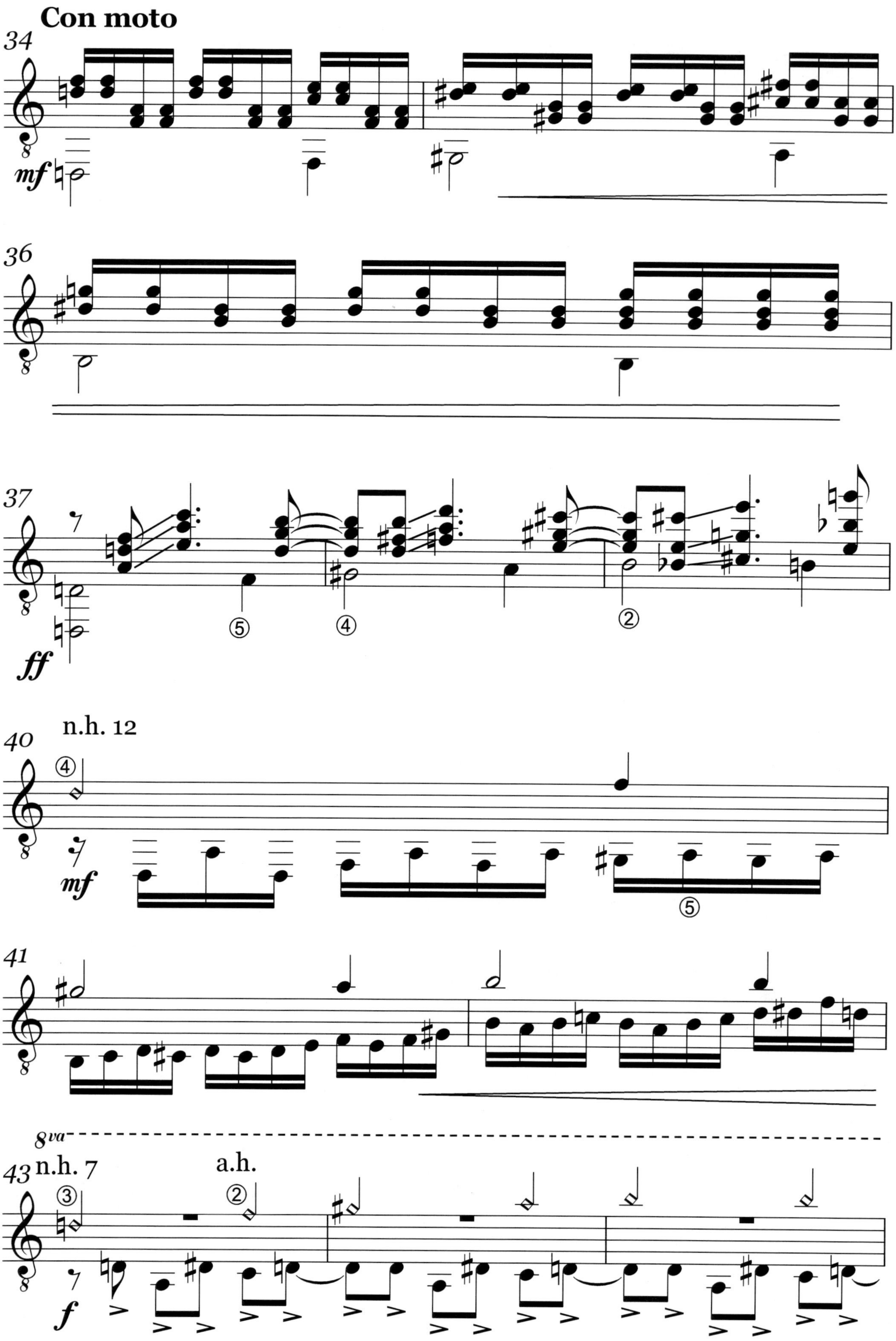
Con moto
34
mf
36
37
ff
40
n.h. 12
mf
41
8va
43
n.h. 7
a.h.
f

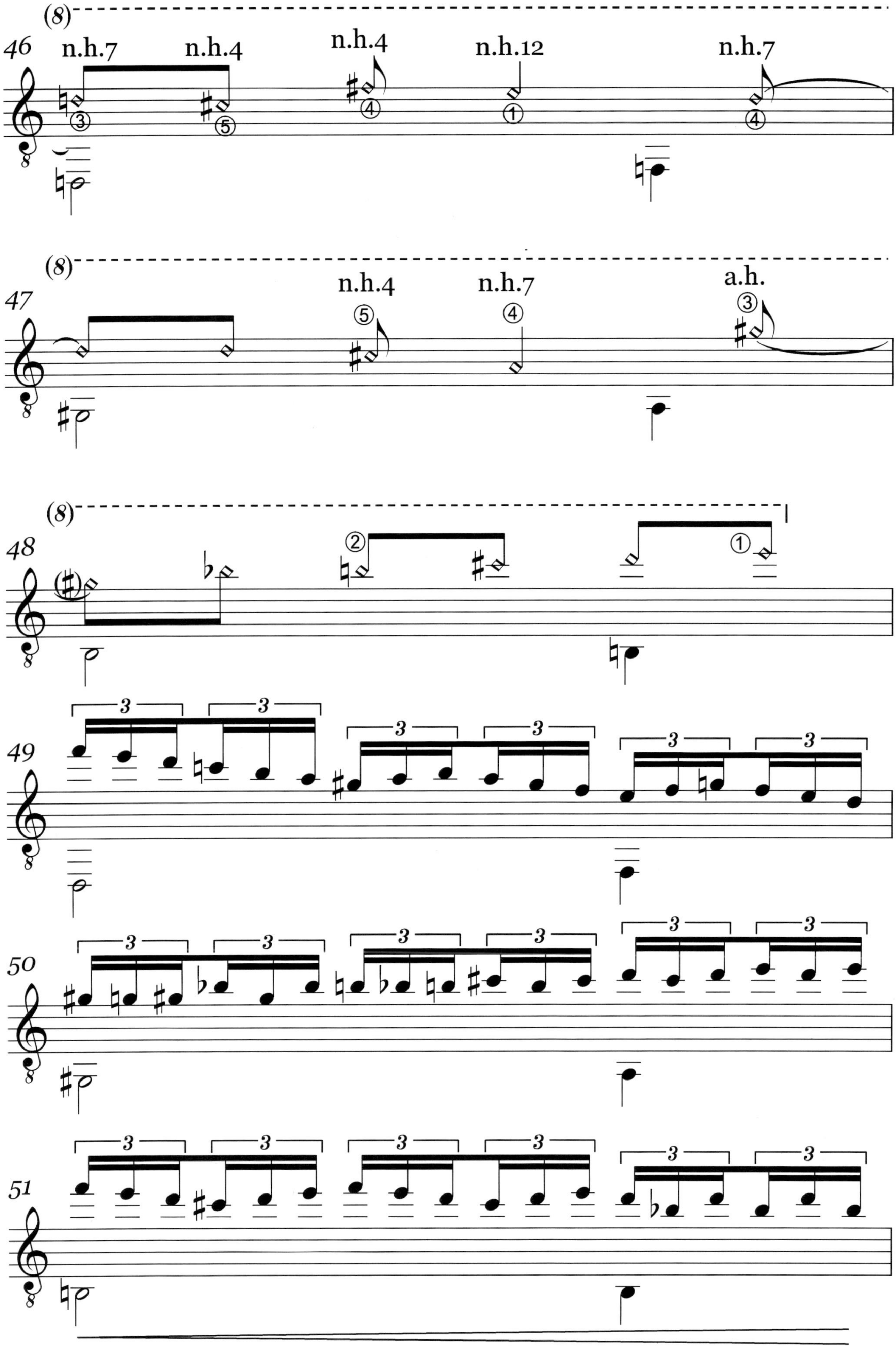
(8)
46
n.h.7
n.h.4
n.h.4
n.h.12
n.h.7
(8)
47
n.h.4
n.h.7
a.h.
(8)
48
49
50
51

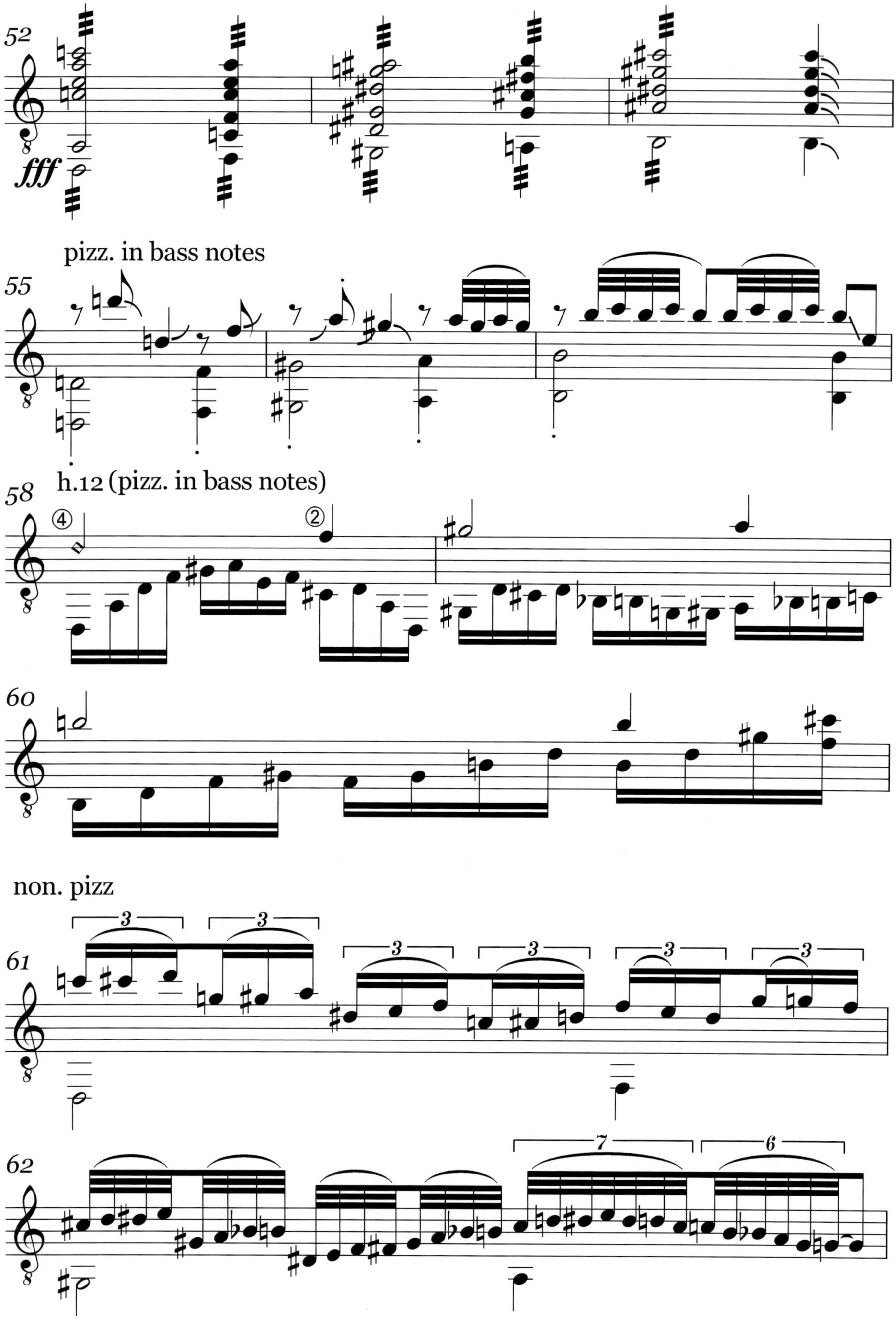
52
fff
pizz. in bass notes
55
58
h.12 (pizz. in bass notes)
60
non. pizz
61
62

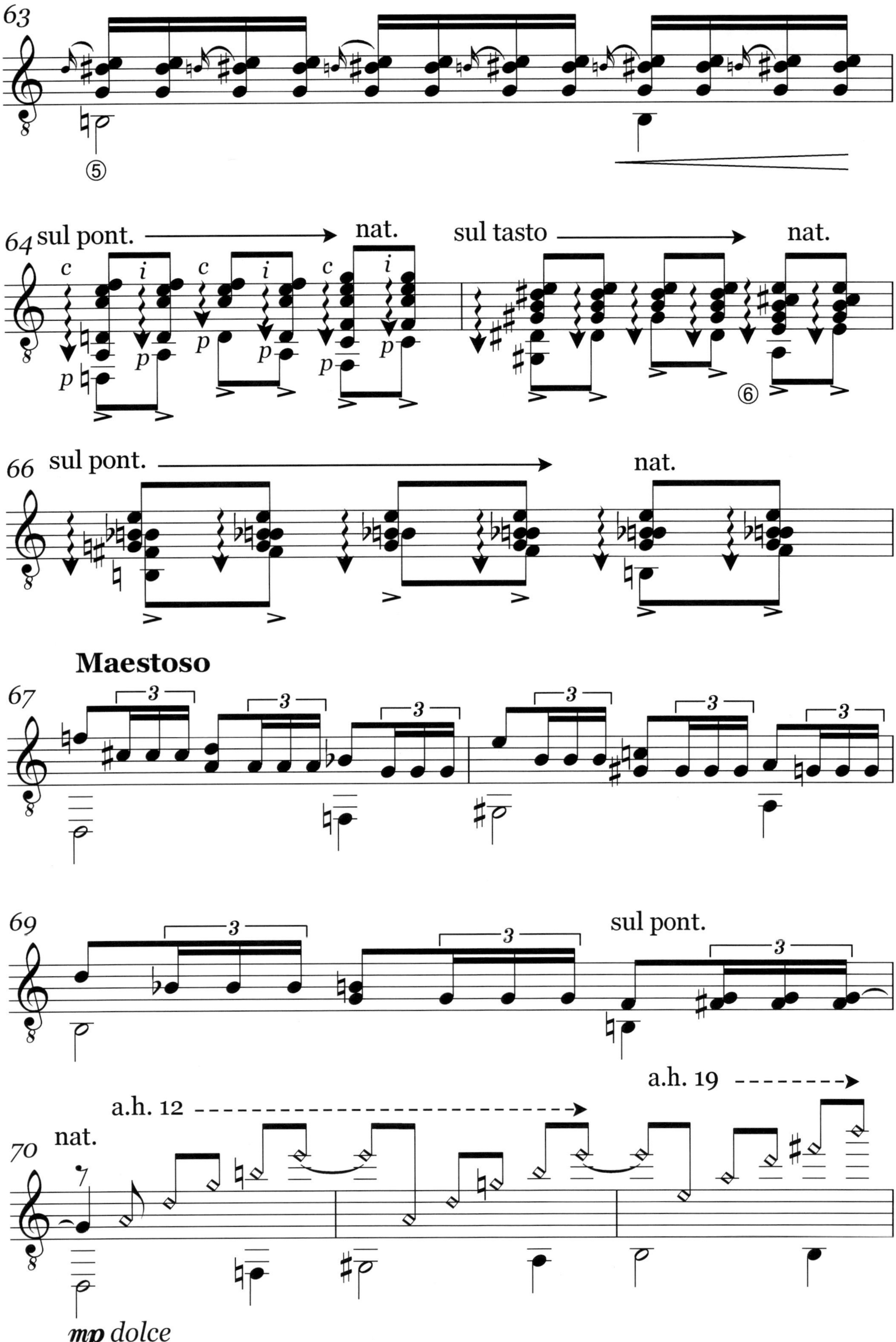
63
64
sul pont.
nat.
sul tasto
nat.
66
sul pont.
nat.
Maestoso
67
69
sul pont.
a.h. 12
a.h. 19
70
nat.
mp dolce

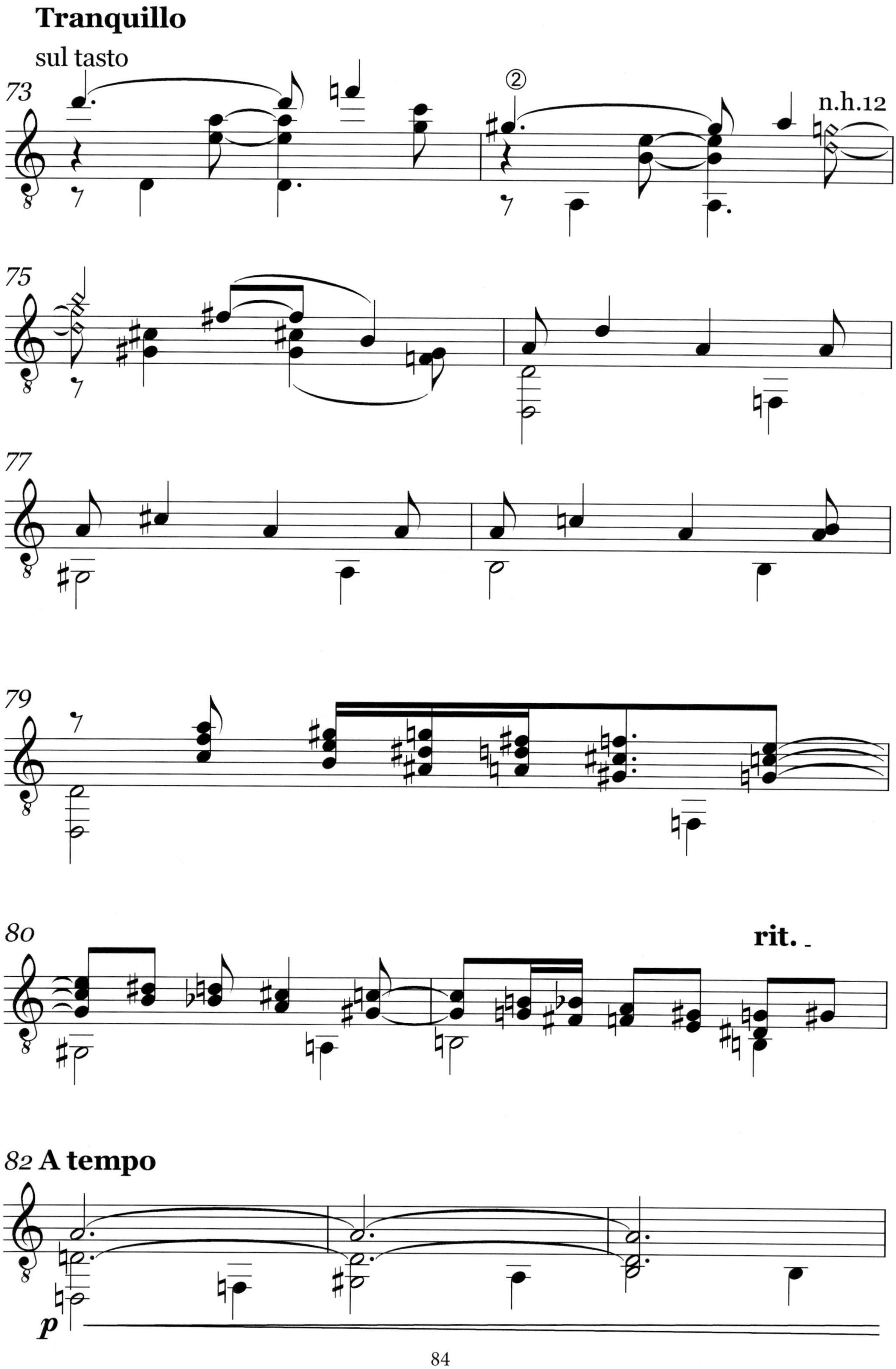
Tranquillo
sul tasto
73
②
n.h.12
75
77
79
80
rit.
82 A tempo
p

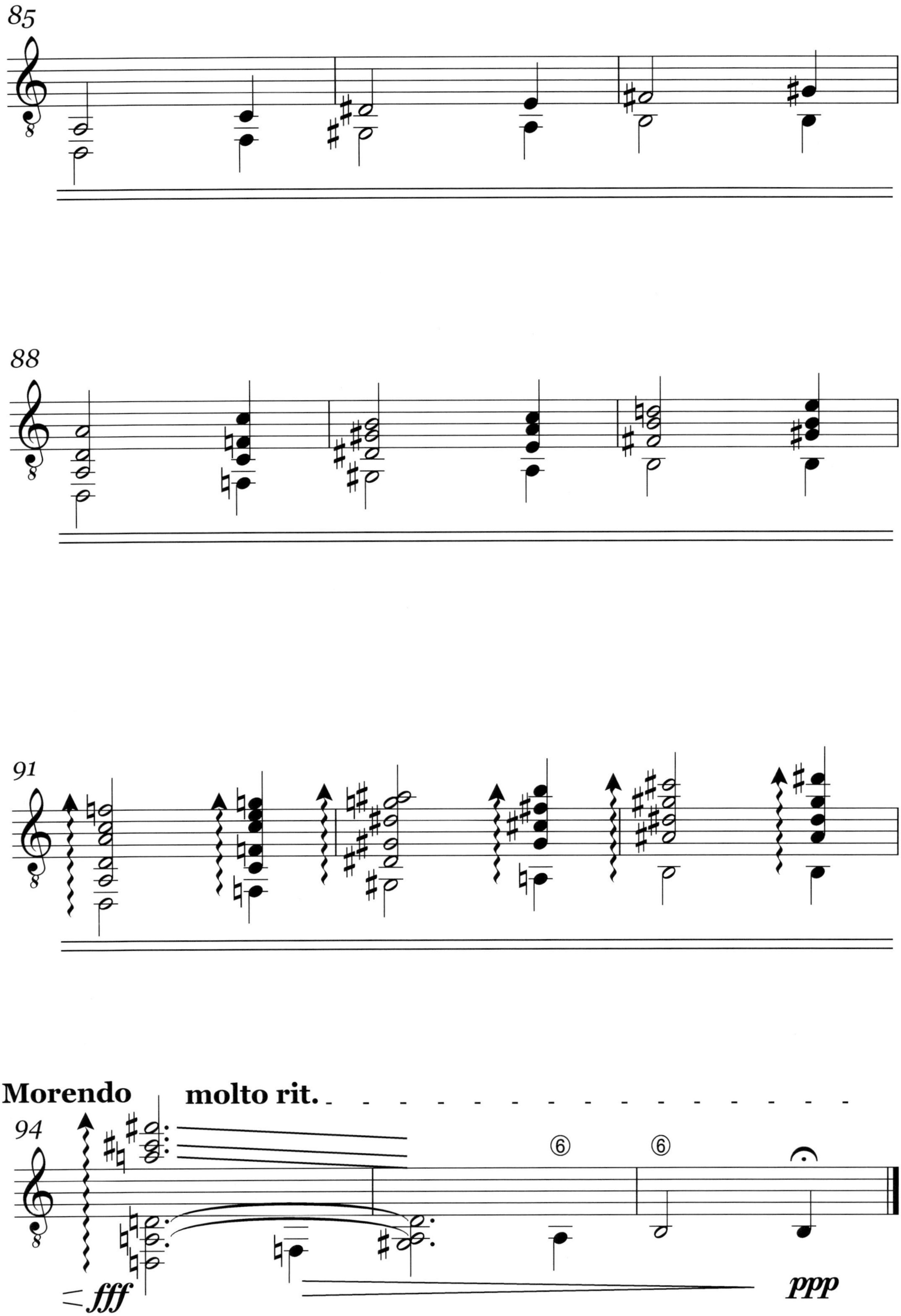
85
88
91
Morendo
molto rit.
94
⑥
⑥
fff
ppp

This page has been left blank to avoid an awkward page turn.

THE MAHATMA OF THE GLEN (2006/2009)

I Grief

II Tears

III Nostalgia

In Memory of James Byrne

The Mahatma of the Glen

I. Grief

Dave Flynn
Composed as a trio in Dublin and Clare 2006
Guitar arrangement made in Spiddal 2009

Optional Tuning: DADGAE
Use open strings where possible

Freely and Spiritually

♩.= circa 50

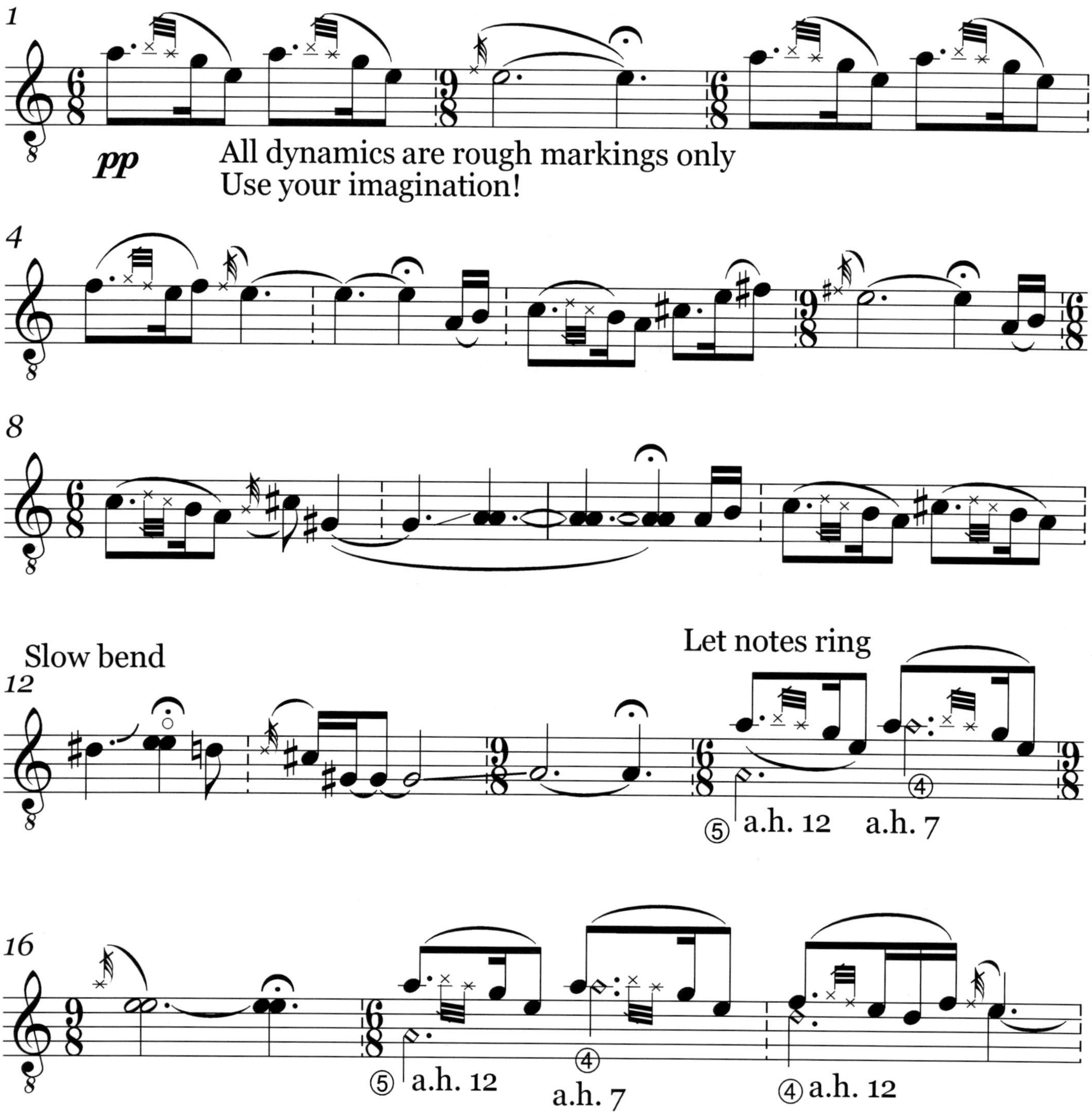

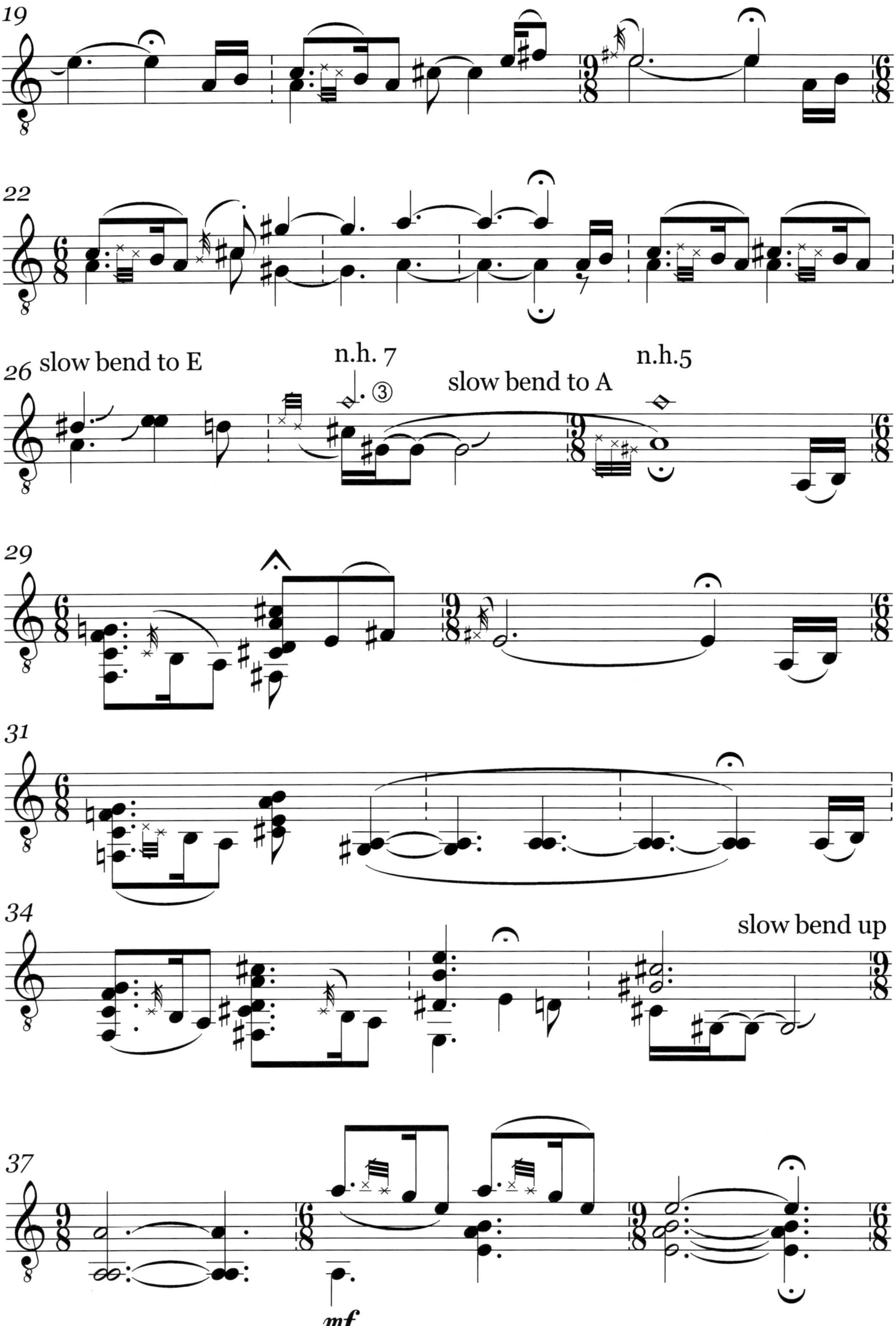
slow bend to E
n.h. 7
slow bend to A
n.h.5
slow bend up
mf

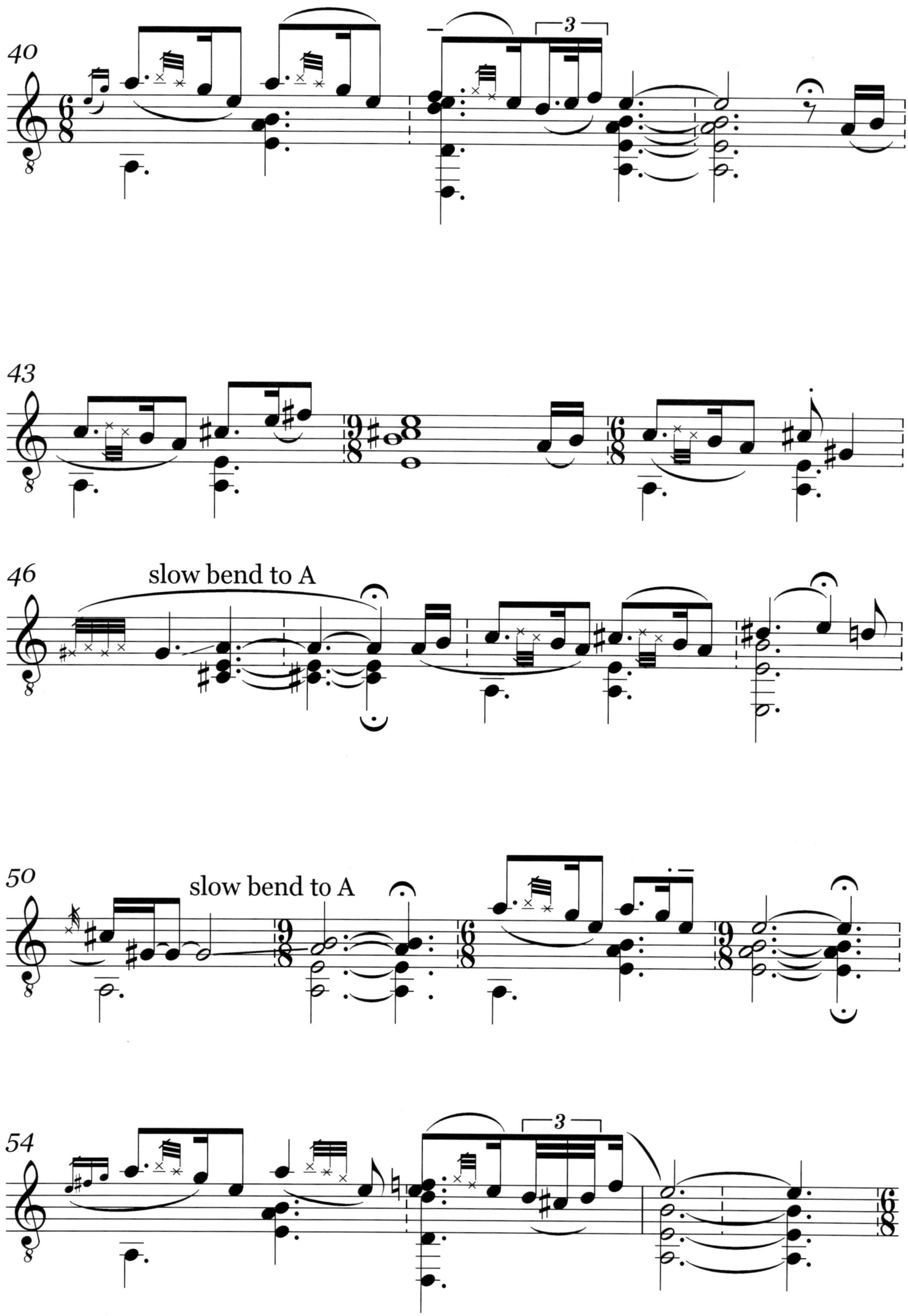
40
43
46
slow bend to A
50
slow bend to A
54

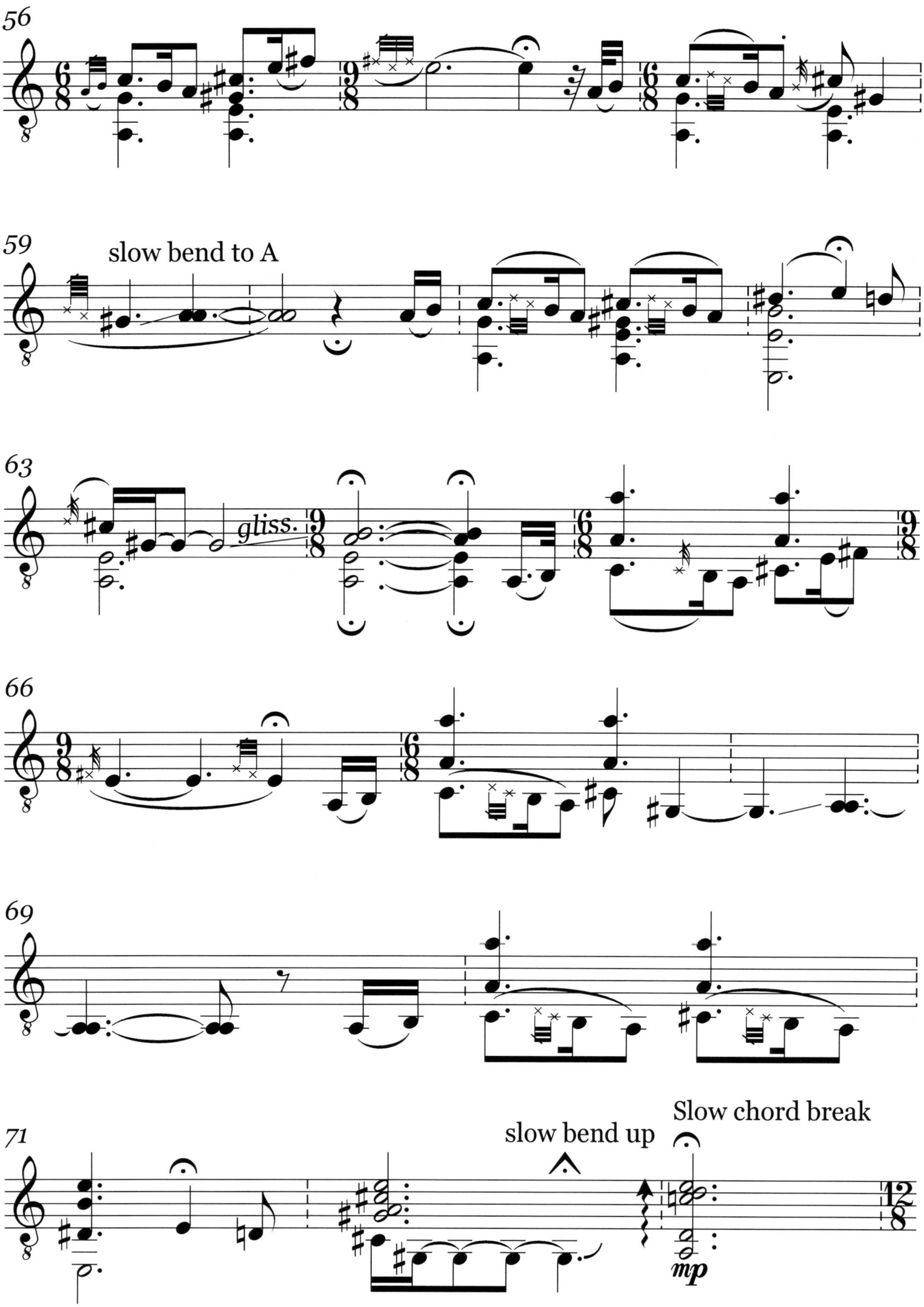
56
59
slow bend to A
63
gliss.
66
69
71
slow bend up
Slow chord break
mp

II. Tears

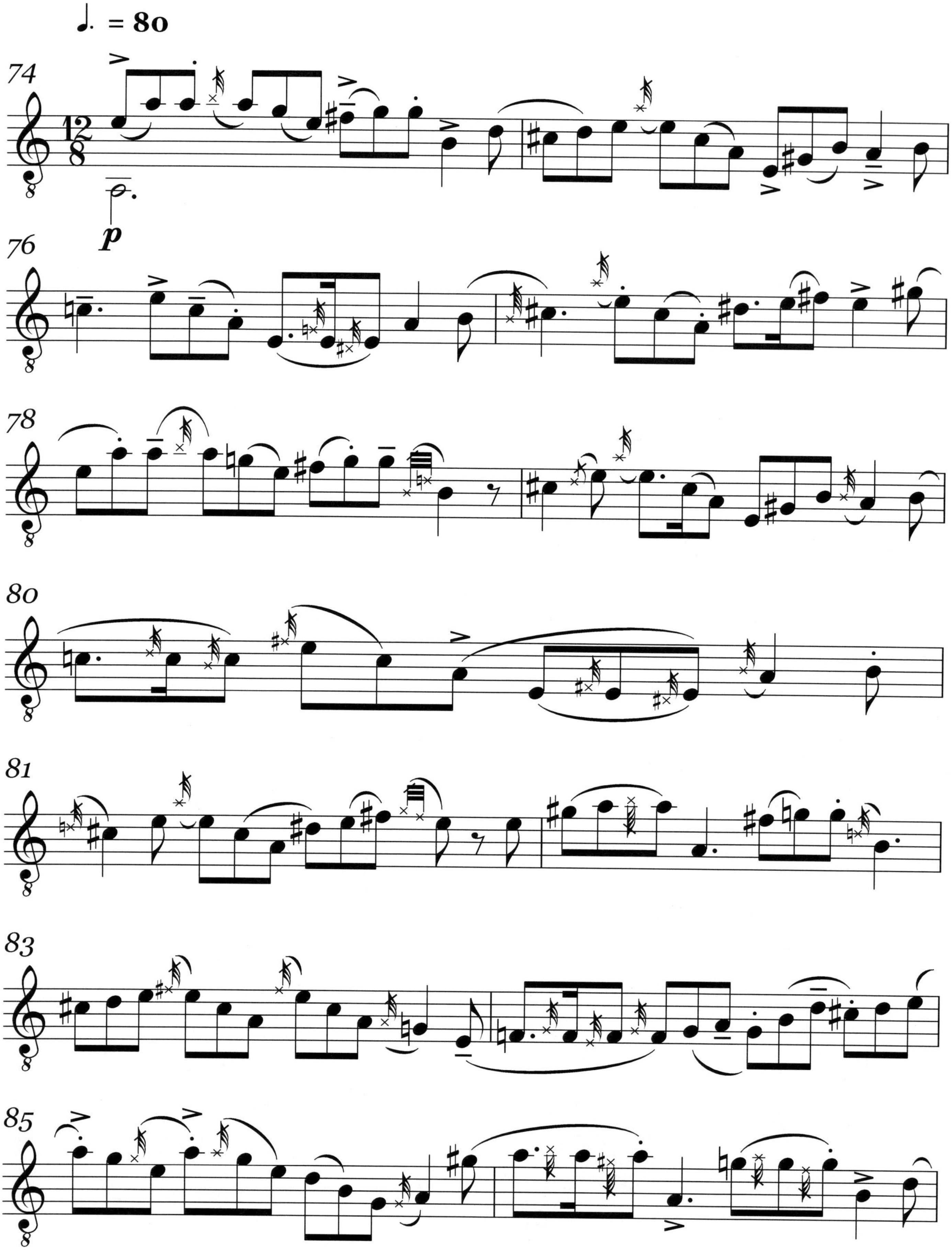

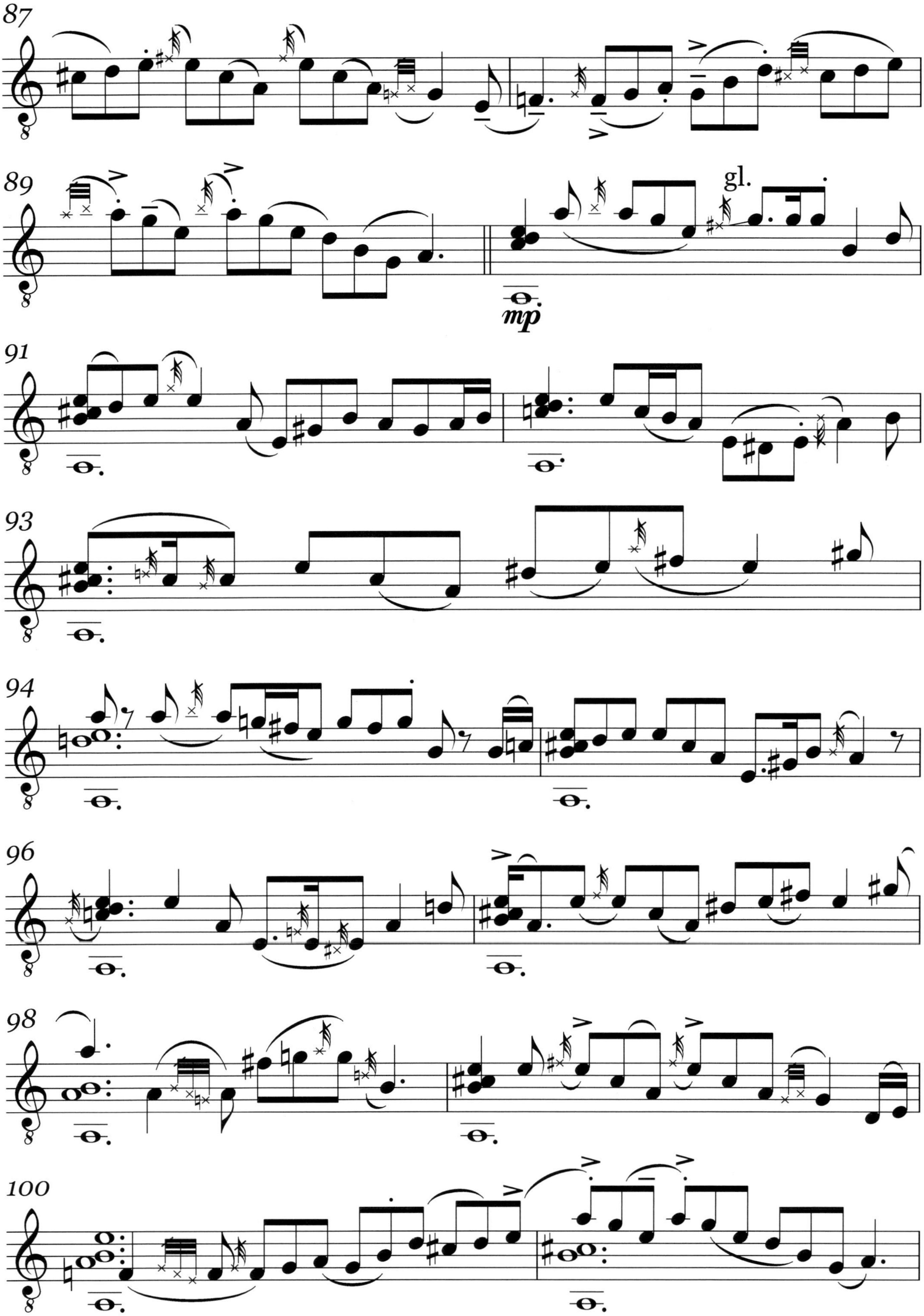
87
89
gl.
mp
91
93
94
96
98
100

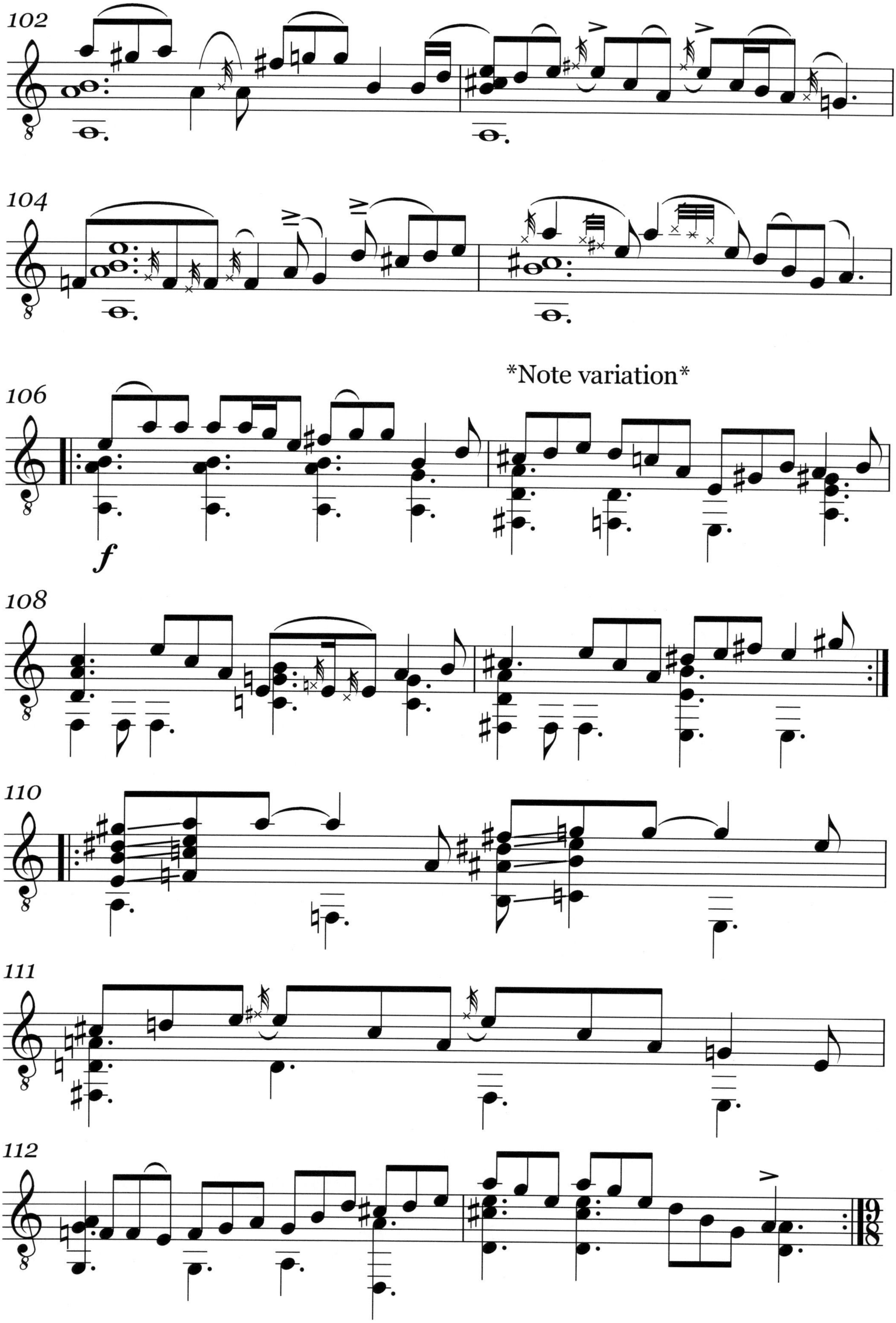
102
104
Note variation
106
f
108
110
111
112

III. Nostalgia

♩. = 150

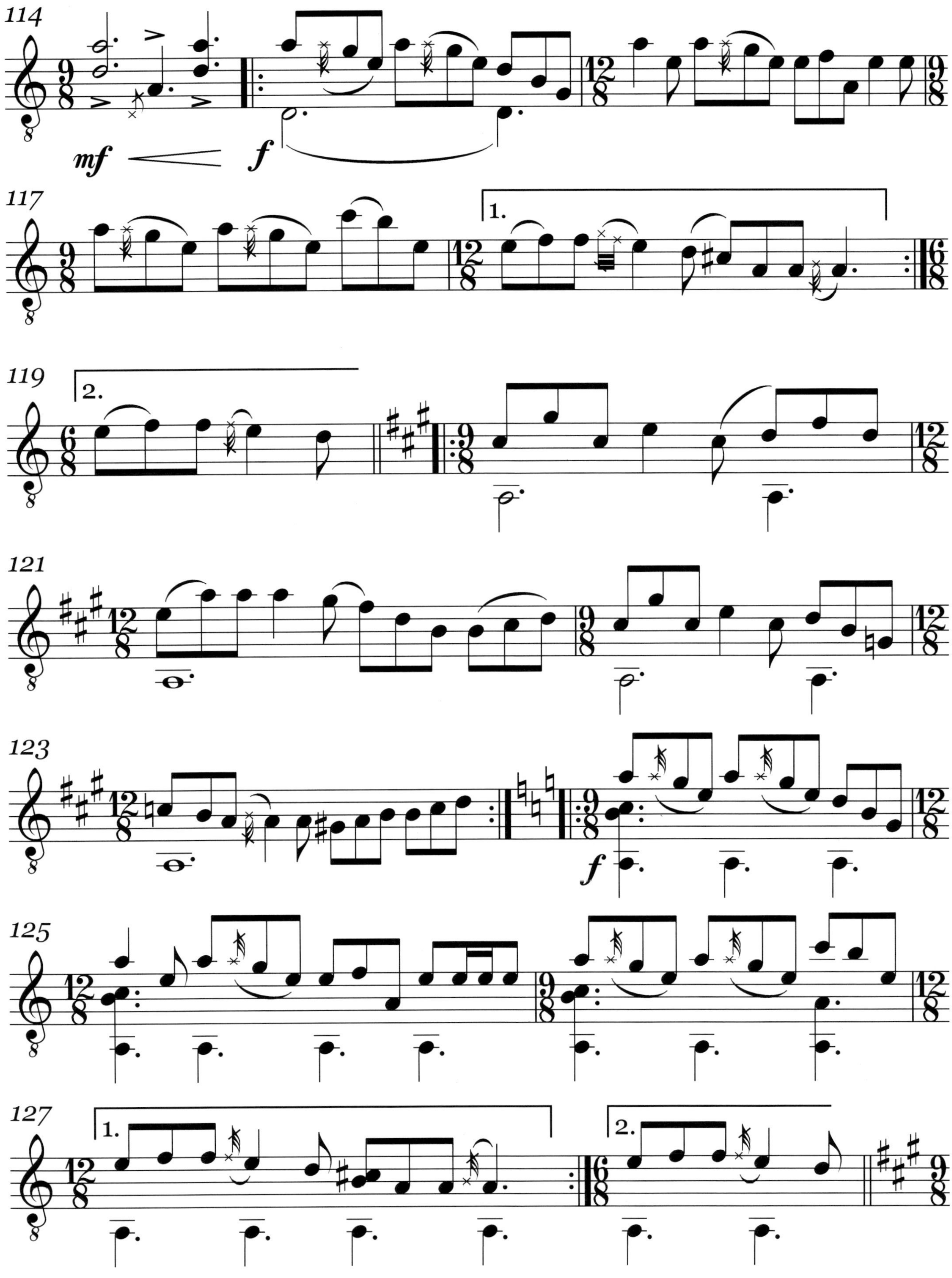

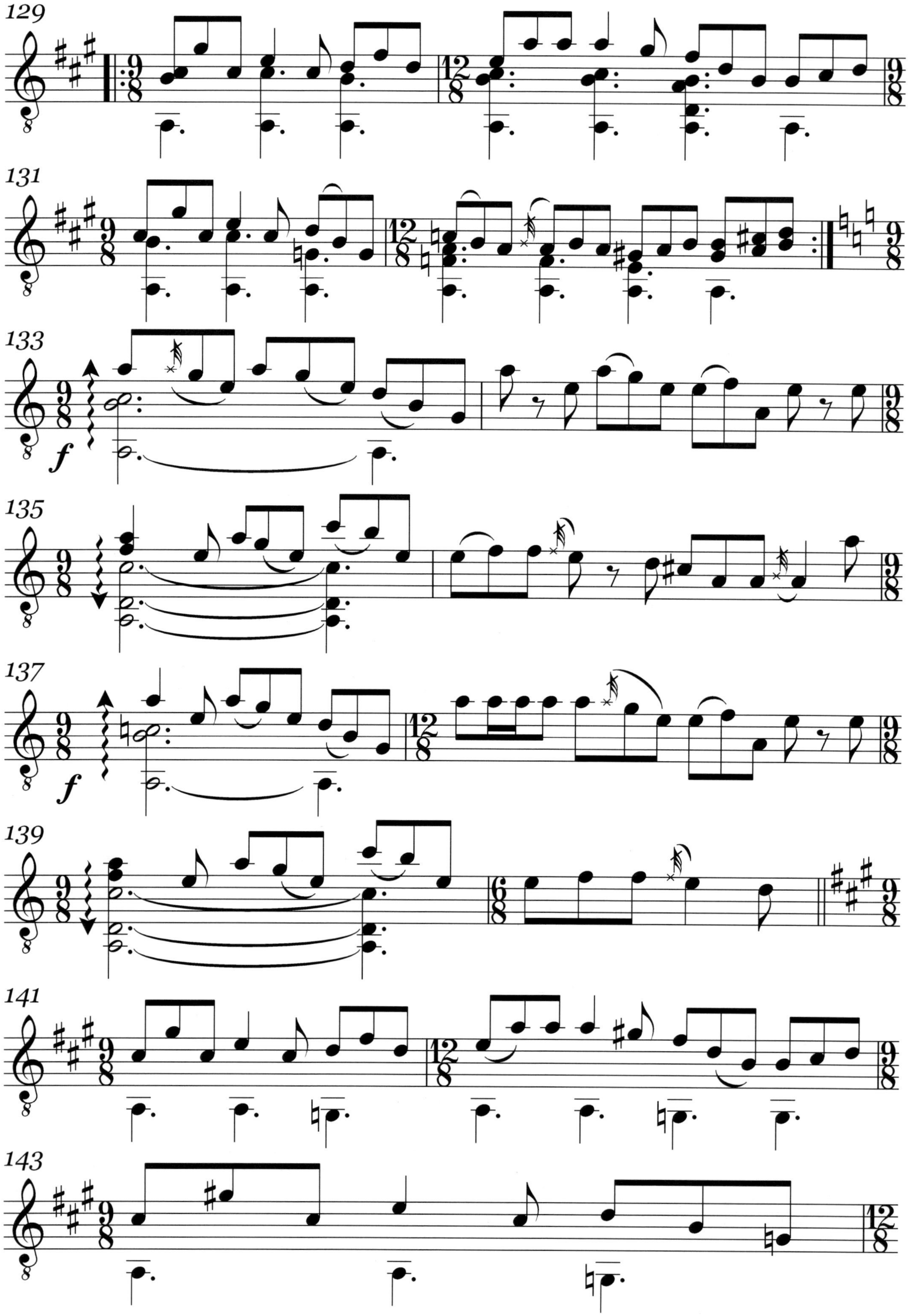
129
131
133
f
135
137
f
139
141
143

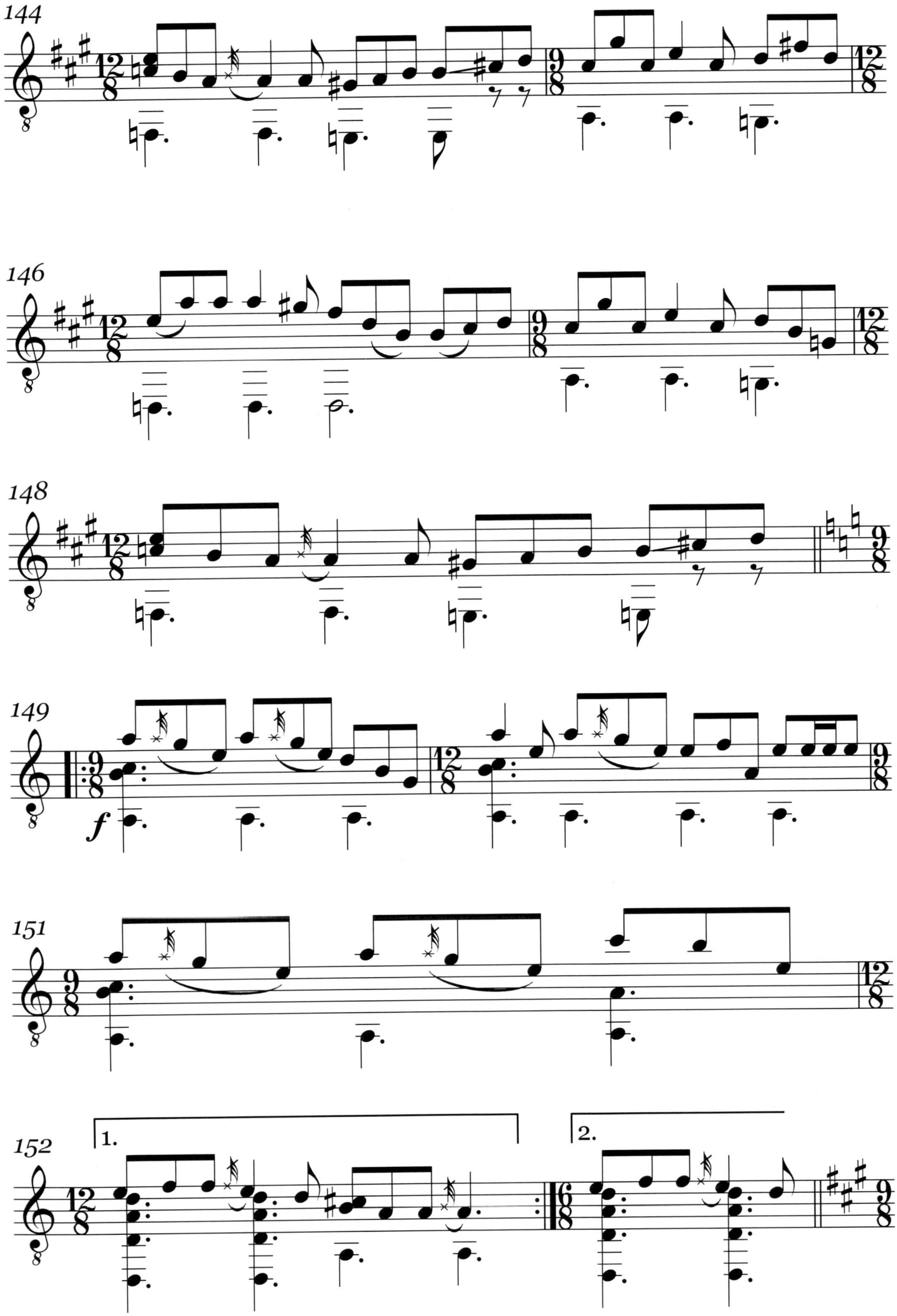
144
146
148
149
151
152
1.
2.

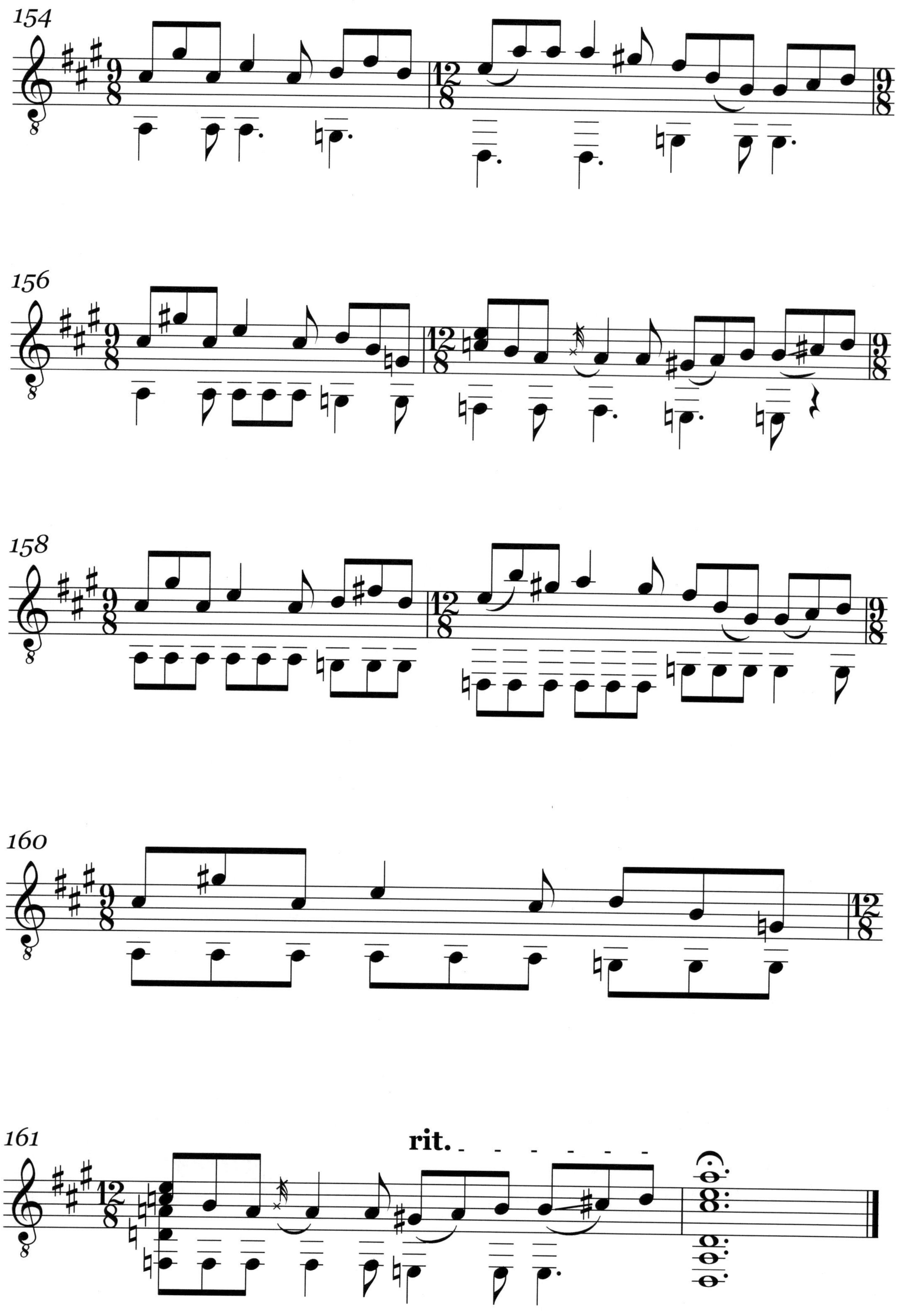
154
156
158
160
161
rit.

“Dave Flynn is a Masterful Guitarist” - Sing Out Magazine

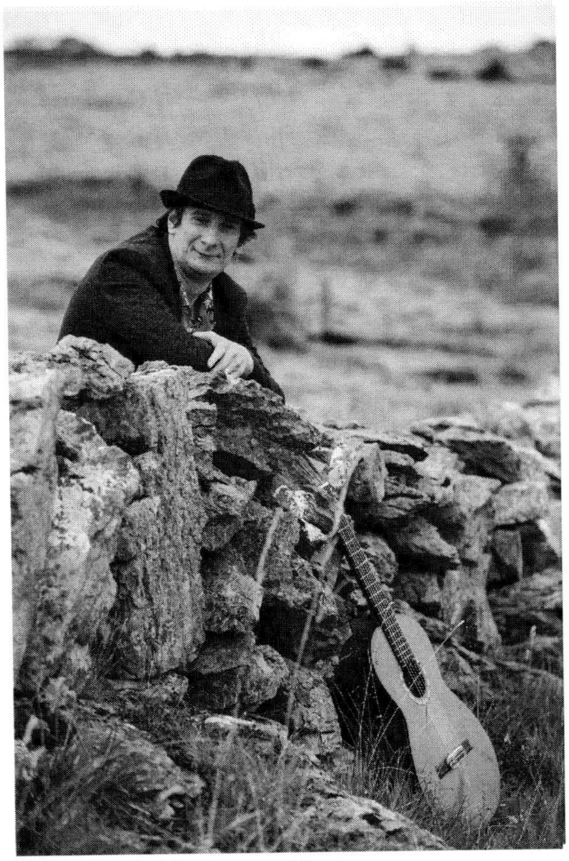

Described as a “genre-jumping genius” (tradreview.com), Dave Flynn is an award-winning guitarist, composer, songwriter and arranger who “occupies a unique position in the world of music.”
(Martin Hayes, *The Gloaming*)

Flynn's expertise in classical guitar, composition and Irish folk music allows him to take audiences on a unique musical journey. He has a distinctive repertoire, mixing stunning arrangements of Irish music and other international styles with compositions praised for their “power and grittiness”. (*The New York Times*)

His solo show, which premiered at the 2010 Edinburgh Fringe Festival, is acclaimed for being “performed with a level of class unparalleled in a lot of folk/classical crossovers.” (*Edinburgh Review, Three Weeks Daily*)

In his solo shows Flynn draws on music from across his acclaimed discography. Central to the show is the unique style he developed for his guitar album *Contemporary Traditional Irish Guitar,* a rare crossover success with classical and folk music critics:

“Releases such as this are a rare and precious resource.” Paul Fowles (*Classical Guitar Magazine*)

Flynn has since toured Europe, Japan and New Zealand with the support of Culture Ireland, in the process giving solo recitals at the Canterbury Folk Festival (New Zealand), the Tournay Irish Music Festival (France) and the Masters of Tradition Festival (Ireland).

As a composer he has been featured at events at the Museum of Modern Art (MoMA) (NYC) and The Kremlin (Moscow). He has twice been the featured composer at the Guitar Festival of Ireland where his music was performed by Clive Carroll, John Feeley and Alec O’Leary. He was the composer-in-residence at the 2019 Classical Guitar Retreat in Scotland, and has performed at guitar festivals in Dundee, Nuertingen, Inishowen, and Clonakilty.

Flynn’s performances with his unique ensemble The Irish Memory Orchestra have led him to appearances at London’s Cadogan Hall, the Sori International Festival (South Korea) and the Moscow Christmas Festival. He has performed with the RTÉ Concert Orchestra at Ireland’s National Concert Hall, once in the Irish premiere of Andriessen’s *De Staat*, and a second time in a concert of his own music.

Initially self-taught, Flynn studied classical guitar with John Feeley and participated in masterclasses with luminaries like Roland Dyens, David Russell and Manuel Barrueco. A former founding member of the Dublin Guitar Quartet, Flynn’s arrangements of Philip Glass’ string quartets brought the group wide acclaim. Glass himself described the arrangements as “really quite beautiful.”

Flynn plays a nylon-string guitar, custom-made by German luthier Frederike Linscheid. His compositions are published by Mel Bay Publications, Reed Music and Frisbee Publications. He holds a PhD from the Dublin Conservatory of Music and Drama, and a Masters in Composition from the Guildhall School of Music and Drama.

www.daveflynn.com

Other Mel Bay Classic Guitar Solo Collections

7 Studies for Guitar (Hull)

24 Pieces for Guitar by Gilbert Isbin (MacKillop)

25 Etudes Esquisses for Guitar (Garcia)

A Tribute to Guitar Masters Vol. 1 (Ramo)

Andrew York: Three Dimensions for Solo Guitar

Anthology of Dimitri Fampas Music for Guitar (E. Fampas)

Classic Koshkin (Koshkin/Koonce)

Contemporary Anthology of Solo Guitar Music (Postlewate)

Contemporary Guitar Composers of the Americas (Multiple Authors)

Contemporary Pieces for Classical Guitar (Jakola)

Conversation Pieces (Long)

Diego Barber Compositions for Classical Guitar

Saints and Fireworks: The Music of Gordon Mizzi Volume Two

Song of the Sea: The Music of Gordon Mizzi Volume One

Guitar Compositions by Carlos Dorado

Homage to Villa-Lobos and Other Compositions (Postlewate)

Introspect (Pellegrin)

Jazz Goes Classic (Multiple Arrangers)

Les reflets de l'obscurite for Classical Guitar (Schwizgebel)

Lyrical Solos (W. Bay)

Master Anthology of New Classic Guitar Solos (Multiple Composers)

Rock Goes Classic (Multiple Arrangers)

Solos for Guitar (F. Hand)

The Contemporary Guitar: An Anthology of New Music (S. Yates)

The Jovicic Collection (Dojcinovic)

Well-Tempered Blues (Beauvais)